Cash Peters has writt[...] a series of educationa[...] fiction books publish[...] awards, mostly for w[...] his time between producing videos and commercials and sponsored series for radio. With Loveday Miller he is involved in a wide range of activities, from personnel selection to police forensic work, connected with *The Telltale Alphabet*.

Loveday Miller works for a large British company, training staff in the use of computers. She has been a practising graphologist for over thirty years. She is a member of the British Academy of Graphologists and of the Graphology Society, and is now seen as a considerable authority on the subject.

THE Telltale Alphabet

CASH PETERS with Loveday Miller

CORGI BOOKS

THE TELLTALE ALPHABET
A CORGI BOOK : 0 552 14325 1

First publication in Great Britain

PRINTING HISTORY
Corgi edition published 1995

Set in 10/12pt. Times
by Falcon Oast Graphic Art, Wallington, Surrey

Corgi Books are published by Transworld Publishers Ltd,
61-63 Uxbridge Road, London W5 5SA,
in Australia by Transworld Publishers (Australia) Pty Ltd,
15-25 Helles Avenue, Moorebank, NSW 2170
and in New Zealand by Transworld Publishers (NZ) Ltd,
3 William Pickering Drive, Albany, Auckland.

Reproduced, printed and bound in Great Britain by
Cox & Wyman Ltd, Reading, Berks.

For my mother,
who said she was right all along.
And she was.

ACKNOWLEDGEMENTS

The development of the Telltale System was an 'organic' process, to put it mildly, and an endurance test for everyone concerned.

Special thanks, therefore, must go out to all the hundreds of people who allowed themselves to be used as guinea-pigs and who played along gamely until we found our feet and got it right. There are simply too many to name, but Damian Christian, Gary Robertson, Diana Luke, Don and Erin Barron, Andrew and Alison Irving, Ian Hardy, Andrew Pooley and Mandy, Mary M, Mary C and Kirstie at MWSP deserve an honorary mention for putting up with it as they did.

Thanks also to Anthony Timson, who breathed life into my computer when it looked set to pack up on me; to James Pinder for his expert knowledge of **R**'s and **Q**'s; to Peter Clapperton for keeping up with the pace when the goal-posts seemed to change virtually every day; to Michael Cohen and Nigel Forsyth at MPC for showing confidence where none had shown it before; and to Averil Ashfield, my editor at Corgi, for her support and judgement, and for remaining so utterly fascinated with the project throughout – a true guiding light.

Oh, and of course thanks to Loveday for her boundless patience, matchless wisdom and endless supplies of bread-and-butter pudding.

CONTENTS

The Telltale System in a Nutshell

'OK, so impress me.'

Well, first let me say that, every so often, an idea comes along which is new. Genuinely new. *So* new, in fact, that it represents a massive advance in current thinking, yet at the same time is so simple that nobody can work out why it hasn't been thought of before.

The material in this book represents just such an idea.

In short, it is a revolutionary system of handwriting analysis, one which goes beyond anything practised by traditional graphologists (indeed, it is completely unknown to most of them), while being so easy to grasp that you can begin using it almost immediately and become proficient in a matter of days.

Armed with only a few key elements of information, you can unlock instantly the behaviour of family, friends, colleagues, even your bank manager – in fact, anyone who ever writes to you – and understand the way they tick. At a single glance, it is possible to learn practically everything about them, from the state of their marriage to how good they are in bed.

I mean, imagine being able to screen a potential romantic partner before becoming involved.

Imagine being told in advance the strengths and weaknesses of business competitors, or of your boss or colleagues, thereby gaining the upper hand in meetings, negotiations and other dealings.

Imagine being just plain sneaky and vetting your loved one's writing to find out how he or she really feels about you.

From Day One, you will know secrets and intimate details about people which, up to now, only they have known. You will see behind the masks they put on and find out what's really going on in their heads. For, while conventional graphology tries to describe the way people function, the Telltale Alphabet explains *why* they do what they do, which is far more useful.

And all you need is a few words on a piece of paper. What could be simpler?

'Hang on, though, I'm just an ordinary person. I've never studied handwriting in my life – but you're saying that even I could do this?'

Absolutely! That's exactly what I'm saying.

We have taught this technique to many people already and

they agree that, once explained, the System is blindingly obvious, consisting as it does of one-third observation, one-third imagination and one-third tiptoeing around stealing scraps of paper from other people's desks!

Above all, it's great fun and will work for anyone prepared to study the Alphabet and decode the telltale meaning of each letter. The more you experiment with it, the better you'll get.

'And this isn't graphology?'

Certainly not! Indeed, I'm *so* sure that it is nothing at all to do with graphology that I am prepared to state the fact in big bold letters.

IT IS NOTHING AT ALL TO DO WITH GRAPHOLOGY.

There.

The contrast with traditional methods of handwriting study could not be greater. For a start, graphology is a science (and many would claim an art) which can only be practised competently after many years of intense study. It is complex and precise and uses a combination of well-tried analytical methods to paint an accurate portrait of the subject. In expert hands, it can be remarkably effective.

Unfortunately, it also has a number of limitations.

Sure, you may discover a few significant details about your partner or employer that you didn't know before, but rarely, if ever, does graphology reach deep into the very soul of a person to discover why he behaves as he does. Questions such as: 'Is this guy spiritually awakened?' or 'Will he cheat me and run off with all my money?' or 'Does my girlfriend really love me?' go unanswered. They have to, because to ascertain such things takes intuition, and until recently most graphologists pooh-poohed the very idea of using intuition to aid them in their work. They saw it as spurious and imprecise. Not reliable enough. Not *scientific*. Whereas for us, intuition – that innate sense of knowing how people function and why they behave as they do – is a crucial factor in the process of interpreting their handwriting.

Furthermore, the old-style analysts have great difficulty working from faxes or photocopies or lined paper; they need a signature too where possible and preferably a page or so of writing to go at before they can reach any satisfactory conclusions.

None of which applies when using the Telltale Alphabet, I'm delighted to say. With our system:

i   the writing can be on anything – lined paper, blackboards, the back of a bus – we don't care;

ii a signature is unnecessary. Of course, it often contains many extra clues to someone's personality but, hey, we can live without it;

iii the writing doesn't have to be an original: faxes and photocopies are most welcome;

iv we don't need reams of paper – a line or two will do. Once I even prepared a three-quarter page of analysis just from the way someone wrote the word 'unfortunately'.

Altogether a much easier, far more relaxed approach, one that can be made to work by anybody in almost any circumstances. In fact, the Telltale principles apply almost universally, so whoever you are and wherever you happen to be in the world, if the guy sitting next to you writes using the standard A-Z alphabet, then you can peer over his shoulder and know everything about him.

'But you still haven't told us how the system works!'

No, you're right, and it's time I did. So here goes.

The Telltale Alphabet

This system is built on a very simple premise: that every letter in the alphabet has its own special significance, and the way you write each letter gives a clue to some facet of your personality. For example, **A**'s show how stressed you are; **p**'s tell us if you're nosy or not; **f**'s and **B**'s indicate whether you are overbearing when expressing your point of view; the size of your **X** shows how committed you are in long-term relationships ... and so on. A little confusing perhaps to begin with, but really it's very logical and you'll soon get the hang of it.

Without exception, and often without realizing it, we are all constantly reaching out to others – for approval, respect, confirmation that we're on the right track in life; to be accepted for who we are and to have our finer points appreciated, our problems understood. Handwriting is one method we use to communicate those needs. And we do it, not just by the words we use, but by the way we choose to write them.

With every fresh stroke of the pen, we drop yet another thread of our life story for someone else to pick up.

We don't think about it, of course, we just write, unaware of the hidden signals we are sending out. But they are there nonetheless, as surely as if we had crafted each letter with great care in order to send a private message to the reader. Every squiggle, loop, dash and doodle vibrates with emotion and screams out, 'This is the real me! This is what I'm like underneath. Please understand me.'

All very dramatic. Or at least it would be, if only we could read the signs.

Well, with the help of this Telltale System we can.

Using the principles laid down in the next few chapters, it is possible to pinpoint a catalogue of character traits, good and bad – everything from generosity, passion, optimism and strength of character, to hopes and ambitions, flaws and failings, deep-seated insecurities and longstanding sexual problems – which, when totalled up, provide a rounded portrait of any writer.

Because it opens up the workings of a person's mind, the System can also pave the way for various forms of personal therapy, by helping to draw to the surface a wide range of psychological problems, stored deep inside, which are holding him back from real fulfilment in life. It may seem a little far-fetched at first, but the process of confronting negative attitudes in this way seems to trigger in some people a fresh perspective on their troubles, transforming the way they think about themselves, even helping to strike a new formula for success and happiness in the future.

The single, most important advantage of this system over traditional graphology is that so much information can be gleaned from so few words in so short a time.

When invited to check out someone's handwriting, I usually get him or her to dash me off a quick sample on a blank sheet of paper. Anything will do, although with all the humility I can muster, I often suggest the names of the authors of this book, Cash Peters and Loveday Miller, simply because, written down, those five words throw up all sorts of juicy intimate details.

Or else, by way of an alternative, it's worth asking for a quick 'Elvis Presley'. Believe it or not, from these two words alone, we can deduce thirteen ...

- not one -

- not ten -

... but a staggering *thirteen* facts about the writer:

- How playful he is in bed
- Whether he appreciates the difference between love and sex
- Whether he is sensible and practical
- If he has a cheery, talkative disposition
- How good is his concentration on the job in hand
- If he is snooty or stuck-up
- If he is stubborn
- If he is easily affronted or put down
- How nosy or curious he can be
- Whether he is 'together' in his head or screwed up
- How he feels about responsibility and commitment
- Whether he enjoys living and has a lust for life
- How much past conflicts and pain affect his present behaviour

Impressed?

OK, supposing I told you that, if the same person were to write a little bit more: say, 'Elvis Aaron Presley – the King of Rock 'n' Roll', you would be able to add at least another *fourteen* facts about him to the above list, making twenty-seven in all – would you be impressed then?

You bet you would. And it's so easy too.

Our Alphabet contains forty-five letters: twenty-six capitals and nineteen lower-case, each one packed to bursting with information.

The reason seven lower-case letters appear to be missing is because these seven when written, are exactly the same shape as their corresponding capitals: **c** and **C**, **x** and **X**, **o** and **O**, etc. Therefore we take it that both, big and small, have identical meanings and, to avoid unnecessary duplication, in each case the twin letter has been omitted. Otherwise, things are just as you'd expect.

'One last point. Surely there must be a thousand variations on each letter. No two people have the same hand-writing, do they? So that must mean I'll need a whole load of expert knowledge before I start.'

Not at all.

You're right, though. There are as many variations on the letters of the alphabet as there are human beings to write them. Luckily, however, they do fall into certain recognizable patterns, which makes our task that much simpler. Later in the book some of the more common ones are provided for reference, together with an explanation of how each letter relates to its neighbours. So somewhere, either in the text or in the mini reference tables at the end of most sections, you should find something approaching the shape of the letter you are looking for.

To really appreciate the ins and outs of the System, you first need a basic understanding of why people behave as they do, and to that end there are three nuggets of background information I'd like to pass on to you. These begin in the next section. Do please forgive me if, at times, the rules seem a little too cut and dried. People are immensely complex, and human nature is such a vast subject with so many thousands of intricate byways to explore, that in order to do it justice (assuming I were able to in the first place!) this book would have to run to ten volumes at least. It doesn't, and we should all be grateful for that.

What follows, therefore, is everything you need to know to get started.

Good luck.

The First Big
Thing You Need to Know

Energy

For many years now, a couple of theatre-going friends and I have been playing a wonderful little game just between ourselves, which I'd like to share with you.

It works like this. Whenever a new musical is due to open in London's West End, the three of us get together over a drink and try to predict how long the show will run for, give or take a few days. Do we sniff a smash hit here or an absolute stinker? Will it sing-and-dance its way triumphantly to the end of the run and perhaps beyond, or close prematurely with near-libellous notices?

It's tremendous fun.

Our game has just one rule: that the verdict must be delivered at least seven days before the first performance – that means prior to the previews and well before the opening night. So that we can't change our minds, we usually deposit a copy of our forecast with the bank and, on occasions, even send a second copy to the producer, labelled 'Not to be opened until the show closes'.

Then we sit back and wait. We read reviews, check the press for any adverse news that might undermine or destroy our prediction; sometimes we've been known to hover nervously outside the theatre box-office counting the number of people in the queue. All in all, I reckon we live and breathe those shows as much as any producer or performer.

Invariably, luck seems to be on our side, however, because, as things currently stand, in the whole time that we have been playing this outrageous game, *we have never been wrong*.

Yet.

Now, that is not to say we won't miscalculate one day. By the law of averages our luck must run out at some point. But even so, our record to date is impressive. Shows may have a long successful run or a brief ignominious one, but in all cases they generally close when we say they will. Often to the day!

So how do we do it? What's the trick? Because if theatre producers and the angels – the name given to their financial backers – could work the same magic and know for sure whether or not they had a hit on their hands, they would never again need to waste all those millions of pounds investing in something that was destined to flop.

In actual fact, there is no real trick to it.

First of all, we grab a poster or leaflet from the theatre, or cut out an advertisement from a newspaper, and examine it. We look at the show's title or logo and the way it is designed, plus any drawings or photos around it. We also take in the colours and the overall tone and layout, and then we ask ourselves, 'Is this pleasing to the eye?' 'Has the idea been thought through properly?' 'Does this production have a good energy to it?' 'Does the poster make me want to hand over hard-earned money to see the show?'

Finally, based on all of that, and with much glee and excitement, we deliver our verdict – 'The show will close on 14th May,' we announce.

And it does.

Usually.

The keyword in all of this, though, is 'energy'.

Every new production has an energy, positive or negative, which is present from conception to birth. You can't see it or touch it because it is given off subliminally, but it's there nonetheless. If it's positive – in other words, if the show is based on a brilliantly original idea backed by plenty of talent and enthusiasm – that same positive energy will continue to be present at every stage from then on, up to and including the design of the poster, thereby increasing the likelihood of the show becoming a success. On the other hand, if the whole idea is a lousy one to begin with, if the feel of it is all wrong, then no amount of effort or money or hype will change that. The show is flawed from the outset and no-one will come.

Now, precisely what constitutes the 'right' energy is a mystery and always will be. Otherwise every production would be a guaranteed smasheroo, wouldn't it? All we do know is that *Phantom of the Opera* and *Miss Saigon* got it right, whilst *Bernadette*, *Leonardo*, *The Hunting of the Snark* and countless other multi-million-pound West End fiascos never did. The angels are still dabbing ointment on their fingers over those, I should imagine.

However, this hidden energy isn't confined to theatre posters, it's everywhere.

For instance, have you ever walked into a room where two people have just had a wild screaming argument? Without a word being spoken, you know that something is wrong – you sense it. There's a deathly silence for one thing. The air hangs heavy with the abuse traded between them, you can almost feel the animosity. It's right there in front of you, like an invisible monster lurking in the room. Immediately, you just want to sneak right back out again and leave them to it.

Similarly, you must have been strolling through town sometime and come across two restaurants right next door to each other – one packed to capacity, loud music playing, staff skipping between tables frantically taking orders, with even more customers joining the queue outside; and the other completely empty. Half the waiters are sitting yawning at the back, while the other half have joined the manager at the entrance to stare enviously at their neighbour's flourishing business.

So how is it that one restaurant prospers while the other drifts slowly into bankruptcy?

On the face of it, the answer would seem to be luck, but it's not really. Examine the situation more closely and you'll find that, in most cases, the quiet business with no customers simply doesn't have an attractive vibe. For whatever reason – gloomy décor, sterile atmosphere, an unhelpful attitude among the staff – the energy is all wrong; passers-by aren't drawn to it. Ask them why and they probably can't give a reason – they just know they would sooner frequent the other restaurant, period.

So you see, there is nothing spooky about the idea of sensing energy. You don't have to be psychic or strange in any way. It's a form of intuition common to us all, one we use regularly without realizing.

And, in the same way, energy is a primary element in the Telltale Alphabet. Whenever we put pen to paper, we are doing two things at the same time:

 i expressing our ideas, thoughts and feelings, and
 ii displaying the energy that underlies those ideas, thoughts and feelings.

You may know nothing whatsoever about a certain individual (and nothing about handwriting either), but by looking at the shape and flow of his words on the page you begin to get a feel for the person behind the pen and can imagine what his character may be like. For instance, if he has a loud, vibrant, larger-than-life personality, you would expect his writing to reflect that. His words will be big and noisy and almost shout out at you from the paper. If, on the other hand, he happens to be reserved and fearful, then his words will be correspondingly tiny, probably backward-sloping too, and somewhat hesitant-looking.

Let me give you an example.

What sort of man would you say this writing belongs to?

I was talking on Saturday

Is he A: a shy, quiet, conscientious shop assistant, or
      B: a bouncy, confident TV personality?

You won't be surprised to learn that B is the answer. The writing is so extrovert, so bursting with life, that it could only belong to someone with bags of positive energy. Naturally, the vibrancy of the inner person gushes directly onto the page.

Here's another. What kind of personality does this person have?

San Francisco with plenty of $.) when
let me know whether you would like the
nuts with the bone — as far as I know

Is he A: quiet, intelligent and reserved, or
      B: flamboyant, fast-talking and cynical?

Please tell me you chose A!

Thank goodness. Because being so cramped and inexpressive, this could only be the product of a thoughtful, low-key nature. Anything else would not make sense.

In short, then, as far as your handwriting is concerned, there is no disguising the kind of person you are inside. Your every last emotion is fused into each squiggle, curl and loop, so no matter how much you may hope to fool people in real life, the truth will out every time.

LEARNING TO WRITE

Most of us learn the basic alphabet at school.

Remember how, to begin with, the letters were completely foreign to you – a few weird and interesting shapes that were fun to finger-paint but a real chore to memorize? You drew them consciously and with great care, thinking hard every step of the way. It was only much later that you came to appreciate how these shapes fitted together in all sorts of fascinating ways to make words and then sentences.

Generally speaking, by the time we reach our mid-teens, such problems are behind us. Writing has become second nature; we scribble words automatically, without really thinking about the look or size of the letters, and also at great speed. The more we scribble, the further we drift from those early nursery-school letter-shapes towards our own individual style. Even if our teachers urge us to write in a particular way – with all the letters sloping forward, for instance – it makes no difference in the end. Bit by bit we will still customize the writing to fit our unique personality, the same way we mould our signature by practising it over and over again until we come up with something suitably adult-looking to put on job-application forms.

By this time, the way we write has become an integral part of our identity, as peculiar to us as our thumbprint. No two handwritings can ever be exactly the same, simply because no two individuals have the exact same history, background, talents, thoughts and feelings. We are all different. What many people don't realize, however, is that subtle changes which creep into our handwriting as we grow older are not the result of age or personality alone, they emerge as a direct response to the events in our life, all of which are stored up unconsciously as we go along, and which then form the basis for future action. The more experience we accumulate, good and bad, and the more we grow and learn and *feel*, the more our writing adapts and matures to reflect those changes.

THE UNCONSCIOUS MIND

Somewhat recklessly, I've mentioned conscious and unconscious behaviour so far without really explaining what they are. It's all very well saying that the energy behind your handwriting flows onto the page directly from experiences stored up in your unconscious mind – but where exactly <u>is</u> it and what is it there for?

Well, to begin with, picture a luxury ocean liner.

Every passenger-ship has two contrasting areas on board: the superficial part above the water-line where the sundecks are, and the swimming-pools, bars, restaurants, cabins and so on; then, beneath the waves, a second, hidden part: the engine-room which powers it all, buried away deep in the bowels of the vessel. Although it may be tucked out of sight, it is by far the more important of the two. For, if the engines fail, the ship will gradually slow down and stop, the lights will go out and everything will grind to a halt. That's how a ship works.

Well, that's also how your mind works – on two levels. The superficial part, above the water-line so to speak, is your conscious mind. This controls everyday activities such as choosing which movie to see on Friday night, selecting food from a menu, deciding how many guests to invite to a house-warming party ... all these actions are undertaken deliberately and with effort, i.e. consciously.

Behind that, though, grinding away non-stop below the water-line, is the unconscious mind: this controls a whole range of invisible functions which happen without your supervising them – for instance, it keeps your heart beating a certain number of times a minute and makes sure the blood pumps around your veins and reminds you to breathe regularly. On top of this, it serves as a storehouse for all your memories, not to mention your morals, instincts and your sense of right and wrong. Even when your conscious mind is asleep, your unconscious is hard at work processing information, filing and storing, preparing you for the day ahead.

(As if all this wasn't baffling enough, there is also the *sub-*conscious mind, which falls somewhere between the two and which handles all those fiddly little jobs that you tend to do without thinking. For instance, it helps you remember how the gears of a car work when you're driving. Gears are tricky to master initially, but in no time at all the process becomes automatic and you seldom give it a second thought after that. The same goes for anything else you do habitually: the way you tie your shoelaces, where you hang your coat when you come home from work, the process of chewing food and swallowing it – all of these are taken care of by your subconscious, leaving you to concentrate on more important things. So in terms of our ocean liner, if I had to rope off an area and label it 'Subconscious Mind', I suppose it would be the staff quarters, the galleys, the service corridors, ducts and pipes or any of the other behind-the-scenes facilities, tucked just out of sight, which make the voyage run that much more smoothly.)

Meanwhile, though, back in the engine-room ... every piece of information deposited in the unconscious mind stays there, and that includes negative or painful memories from the past. Every disappointment, every resentful thought, every feeling of envy or bitterness, jealousy or low self-esteem ... they all remain in place, churning away below deck, deep down and out of sight. So far down, in fact, that we might not even be aware of their existence. Some may date back as far as childhood, others may have been caused by more recent events, such as a messy divorce or a long-term family dispute; but whatever lies at the root of these troublesome memories, as long as the problem goes unresolved, the legacy of it continues to lurk in the back of our mind until we are prepared to confront the issues and defuse the pain surrounding them.

But why *should* we confront them? Emotional traumas are difficult enough to handle the first time around – the last thing we want to do is resurrect ancient grievances and live through them a second time.

'What's done is done,' we say, wiping our hands of them. 'Let sleeping dogs lie.'

But they won't lie, that's the trouble.

Left untended, they continue to cast a grey shadow over our life.

Example 1: In the past five years Janice has had three serious relationships go wrong. She was committed heart and soul, but each time her partner cheated on her, leaving her with feelings of bitterness and self-doubt. Now, faced with launching into a fourth relationship, she finds herself half-expecting the same thing to happen again. She tries to fight it, but can't help herself. Her perspective on love has been distorted badly by those doomed experiences in the past.

If, like Janice, we open up emotionally and allow ourselves to be vulnerable, and in consequence someone takes advantage, hurting our feelings along the way, that sense of disillusionment never really goes away. Instead, from then on, we use memories of the experience, stored up in our unconscious mind, as a filter through which all similar situations will be viewed. Result: we stop trusting others quite so readily and eventually grow cynical of their motives.

Example 2: When Dan was seventeen years old, a police officer arrested him wrongly and on the flimsiest of pretexts, causing untold distress to him and his family and generating a profound sense of distrust and injustice which has remained with him ever since. These days, the moment he spots a police officer he is immediately on the alert, fearing a repetition, even though this apprehension is, for the most part, completely unfounded.

Example 3: As a small child, John reached through a garden gate to stroke an Alsatian dog. It turned nasty and bit his wrist almost through to the bone. No wonder, then, that he is still wary of large dogs several years on. Those gruesome memories – pain, fear, betrayal – remain powerful impulses, so that now when he sees a dog, even a friendly playful one, he finds himself living in fear of the incident repeating itself.

These are just random examples of wounds that haven't healed. Your own life will have thrown up dozens more, I'm sure. As you grow older, troublesome incidents from the past get jumbled up with all the pleasurable and beautiful ones and the memories, painful or otherwise, are then woven intricately into your handwriting. Unjumbling them is what this Telltale System is all about.

Later on, we'll demonstrate precisely how it works. For now, let me offer a couple of illustrations.

JAKE

He's a young man who, though extremely bright, had an uncertain childhood. His parents were both violent alcoholics, and records show that they beat him and abused him regularly before eventually abandoning him; consequently he spent most of his early teen years in care, being shunted from institution to institution without proper love or attention. He has no job and no prospect of ever getting one. He often contemplates ending it all.

Jake writes like this:

Fifteen copies could be available but the stores Told me that fifteen would be

You don't need to know anything about handwriting analysis to see that there is something very disturbed about that. Note the confusion here, the mixture of capitals and lower case, the shaky and uncertain way his words stumble across the page. The man is fighting accumulated pain from his past. Each episode registers as a glitch on his unconscious, and every one of those glitches has been worked into the handwriting.

At some time in the future Jake may emerge from this trough and realize that life throws up wonderful days as well as rough ones. Hopefully, as he matures and his attitude changes, then his handwriting will change with it. In the meantime, as long as he stores up feelings of anger, rejection, bitterness and disillusionment, this latent negative energy is infused into every mark on the page.

Now, in stark contrast, take a young woman from a more stable background.

SUZIE

She grew up in a warm, loving environment with affectionate, attentive parents who lavished every possible luxury upon her, including a first-class education. Very soon she will be leaving college, poised for her first job – a balanced, stable, caring, confident individual.

Life hasn't always been a bed of roses for Suzie. She will undoubtedly have suffered a few tumbles and disappointments as she grew up – we all do. Nevertheless, she ventures out into the world feeling positive and expecting great things. Her writing looks like this:

With just a quick glance, you can sense the vibrancy here, and this positive energy filters through into all other aspects of her demeanour: the way she dresses, the way she treats others, the tone of her conversation and the attitude she brings to her work. But whether the energy is positive, or negative as in Jake's case, it will always spring out at you from the writing, just as it does from those theatre posters in our little predictions game.

No matter how the personality of the writer manifests itself in life, those same impulses will be present in the way he forms his words on the page. As unlikely as this might seem to you right now, in drawing each letter of the alphabet, we echo the gesture we would make in expressing that same emotion with our body.

Later on, we'll discover how a capital **P**, for example, reveals a person's level of curiosity in the world around him. If you picture the **P** as a stem with a snout on the top, like this: , then the nosier the writer is, the larger the snout will be.

Again, take the letter **V**.

V's relate to sexual experience. In a sitting position, if you look down, you can see that your thighs form a **V**-shape. A sexually confident individual will draw his **V** with the thighs spread out: $\bigvee$, because he feels relaxed around the subject and knows there is nothing to be inhibited about. A shy, inexperienced lover, on the other hand, will always have a tightly-clenched **V**: $\bigvee$. The 'thighs' are closed because the writer has not yet come to terms with the full power of his sexuality and lacks confidence when going to bed with partners.

Sceptics will dismiss this immediately as pure coincidence. Well, if so, then it's a coincidence which repeats itself over and over again.

For myself, having witnessed the System in operation countless times, it makes sense to me that, for each of us, our energy flows into everything we do – the way we walk, dress, talk, our approach to social events, work and play – including, and especially, the way we write.

But there is more to handwriting than just energy. We also bring to it the wealth of our life experience, as we were saying earlier.

We are moulded for ever by the early years of our upbringing: the surroundings, the people we hang out with, our parents' attitude and opinions, the newspapers we read, whether we're rich or poor, privately- or State-educated, the religion we are introduced to, and a whole load of other data, such as language, etiquette and specialist knowledge, that we take on board as we grow up.

But does this conditioning serve to endorse who we really are and thereby enable us to fulfil our true role in life, or is it just a way of making us conform to what everyone else is doing?

This is the second big thing you need to know.

The Second Big Thing You Need to Know

Duality

Another good reason for learning the Telltale Alphabet is that it enables you to vet possible romantic partners and know in advance whether they really are everything they seem to be. For that alone, it's well worth the price of this book, believe me.

Anyone who has ever placed an advertisement in the Lonely Hearts column will recall that nerve-racking moment when a batch of replies drops through the letter-box.

Eagerly, you rip them open one by one, only to find that every single person turns out to be completely unsuitable. Not only are the photos dreadful, but the letters are tacky too, and packed with the most inappropriate sentiments. Worst of all, every respondent seems to have either totally misread your ad, or else taken on board your requirements and then carefully manipulated their own character traits to fit the description.

It can be a harrowing experience, though one which teaches a valuable lesson in life, namely: people often lie to you about themselves.

More than that, they lie to *themselves* about themselves.

Most of us, it seems, carry a distorted view of who we really are. You must have read newspaper stories about painfully anorexic women who stare into the mirror every morning and still see a fat person standing there. Or men with dazzling male-model looks who are completely screwed up because they have a penis of below average size. To compensate, they drive big red cars and joke about how good they are in bed, and smoke Cuban cigars as long as your arm. But underneath all the flash and glamour, their self-confidence is in tatters.

Thanks to the media – especially TV commercials and glossy magazines which set impossible images for us to imitate and live up to – we're made to feel that the person we are inside is somehow not good enough, it falls short of what is expected of us. And so to make ourselves more acceptable and conceal any weaknesses, we construct a clever façade.

A friend of mine in Santa Monica, California, relates a scary tale concerning his wife and one of her early dating experiences.

She had placed an advert in a Lonely Hearts column which attracted dozens of responses. Having sorted out all the losers, loners and liars who replied, she chose one chap who lived a few miles up the coast and whom she rather liked the sound of. In the photo he was blond, clean-shaven and looked friendly enough. Furthermore, in the accompanying letter he said he was six feet tall, gentle and kind with an interest in nature, particularly moths and butterflies – all of which sounded extremely appealing to her. So the next day she called up and they arranged to get together in a local restaurant.

On meeting him, she found him to be quite a nice guy –

soft-spoken, very affectionate – though a tad shorter than expected, at only 5'7". He'd also grown a beard since the photograph was taken. But never mind, she thought. He seemed kind and caring enough, and everything was going fine, so what the heck?

Indeed, things *were* fine. They chatted and drank amicably until after the dessert, when, quite suddenly, he reached across the table in full view of the other customers, grabbed her shoulders and began shaking her roughly until she agreed to another date with him.

Wisely, she didn't. She scooped up her belongings there and then and fled the restaurant! What a maniac!

But you see what I mean?

In his own mind, that guy probably considered himself to be a decent, law-abiding soul. When he looked in the mirror he *was* nearly six foot, not 5'7". And that silly shoulder-grabbing stunt was merely a joke taken too far. But, of course, my friend saw none of this. To her, he was nothing but a liar and an unruly brute. The inside and the outside just didn't tally.

We human beings, almost as part of our education, learn how to put on an acceptable front. It's the quickest and easiest way to ensure that we fit comfortably into society and don't get branded as oddballs or freaks. The only way to penetrate this kind of carefully-erected shield and see what is really going on behind, is by taking a close look at the way the person writes. People can lie, looks can lie, even cameras can lie, but handwriting never does.

So, as well as **feeling the energy** given off by the written word, you also need to be on the lookout for signs of **duality**. These occur either when someone is putting on an outer display, as in the above example, in order to prevent others from seeing the real person underneath, or else when seeds of self-doubt sown during childhood cause a person to behave in a way which pleases other people but does not conform with his true nature and so prevents him from achieving his full potential later on in life.

'Hmmm, I'm not so sure I follow this. Perhaps you could do me a favour and give an example.'

Actually, I'll do better than that, I'll give you two.

JANE

Jane is a schoolteacher. She is middle-aged and happily married with two young children, a mortgage and several loan repayments to keep up, not to mention a whole load of other commitments. However, she is generally contented with all aspects of her life. Well, all except one.

When she was younger she had just one motivating ambition: to be a fashion designer. As a teenager it was her only interest and she felt sure she was destined to make a career of it. But her parents thought differently. In their eyes, designing was much too precarious a profession. Very risky, with an extremely high failure rate. Teaching would be far more secure, they said.

Stupidly, Jane listened to their advice and suppressed her dreams.

These days, she bitterly regrets the decision and could kick herself for not following her own instincts. She sees teaching as uncreative and, as she becomes increasingly bored and frustrated, she finds herself yearning once again to be a fashion designer. This sense of having 'made a wrong turn' permeates her entire life, yet she feels it is far too late to remedy the situation.

Jane's handwriting looks like this:

Talk to me about

Notice the way the upright stems on the **k**, the **l** and the second **t** are split to the very top. In every case, the back of each letter is peeling away from the front of it – a telltale sign of duality, of the conflict between one set of values or ambitions and another. In Jane's case, the deep desire to be creative is pulling her one way, while her ongoing responsibilities to her family as well as the instructions given to her by her parents are pulling her the other.

From our teen years onward, the main problem facing us all is to decide what our proper course in life should be. It can be a real puzzle. Which path will lead to personal, spiritual, mental and emotional fulfilment, and which one will steer us way off course towards a dead end, where, instead of being who we really are and achieving our potential through positive action, we settle for mediocrity, survival, the basics – putting on a contented face that says 'I'm happy being part of the crowd', living out another person's vision of what is best for us while all the time, deep down inside, there lurks a unique individual struggling to get out. Finding our true self is a matter of trial and error, and very often we take a wrong turning.

Let me tell you the story of Eddie Average. It's a simplistic little yarn, and yet one that must ring true for many millions of people.

EDDIE AVERAGE – A LIFE?

This is Eddie. He's a forty-four-year-old government officer who has just been passed over for promotion for the third time. And here is his handwriting:

enclosed my manuscript work

Pause for a moment and take a good look. Again, until we reach the Alphabet we remain unable to decipher the code built into the words, but without even knowing the specifics, just the tone and the feel of the writing, its smallness, the lack of energy and the way it dribbles across the page, should tell you more than enough about the guy even at this early stage.

Eddie is feeling more and more at odds with his chosen path through life. Where did he go wrong? What happened to all those burning ambitions he nursed as a teenager? To be a professional jazz musician, to travel the world, to drive a Rolls-Royce Corniche ... how come he fell by the wayside?

Here's how.

Phase One

All babies are born with a clean slate.

In the beginning, Eddie had no beliefs, no prejudices, no fears, no conscience, no concept of what was healthy or harmful, forbidden or permissible; no checklist of moral values, no sense of duty or responsibility. Apart from a few raw basics – personality, sexuality, his looks and a certain will to survive – all this extra mind-baggage was accumulated while he was growing up.

His parents started the ball rolling by introducing him to basic language as well as the delights of personal hygiene, discipline, good manners, family arguments, God, education and leisure activities. Later on, when he attended school, a new catalogue of values was added to these by his teachers and classmates.

At seven years old, Eddie's handwriting looked like this:

little—Red—Riding —Hood what big eyes

Somewhat undisciplined perhaps, but free-flowing and highly individual. All the signs show that he was an outgoing boy with bags of vitality and imagination.

Phase Two

In next to no time, he was watching TV and movies, reading books and comics, talking freely to other children and picking up views and attitudes from them.

The older he got, the more he pieced together an acceptable pattern of behaviour for himself, one which, hopefully, would win him friends and approval and not alienate too many people. In short, he learned to conform and be pleasant and fit in. He played for the college football team, acted in a couple of Shakespeares, passed a few exams, grew his hair, became a socialist, learned to play the trumpet, did everything else that was expected of him and generally laid the foundations for being a fine, upstanding member of society.

In one respect, though, Eddie differed from the rest. Throughout his youth he nursed a tantalizing dream: to be a professional jazz musician. Friends mocked the idea, his tutors laughed it off as a pipe-dream, but Eddie was determined. Alas, since professional engagements were a little scarce at the time he left college, he was forced to take a regular desk-job until the Big One came along.

So far so good.

But then something else happened. Something not so good.

Along came Reality. The Way Things Are. *The System*.

Phase Three

Now, The System is rather like a steamroller. Take your eyes off it for a second and it will roll right over you and flatten you into conformity.

Before it flattens you, though, it offers you a trade. In return for crushing your spirit, wiping out your wilder dreams and pigeon-holing you under 'N' for Normal, it undertakes to provide you with a stable lifestyle – nice home, job, car, security and hardly any risk at all. That way your place in society is guaranteed as well as all the trappings that go with it, from video recorders to microwave ovens. To be normal, all you have to do is abandon your wilder hopes and aspirations and work at a job you don't really want to do. That's all.

Don't laugh – the world is full of people who made this trade: cab-drivers who wish they'd become interior designers – 'I'd give anything to live my life over and try it'; accountants who feel they were born to be airline pilots but never gave it a shot – 'Too risky – didn't have the dedication'; traffic wardens who, once upon a time, intended to train as professional dancers – but that was long ago, before they had a family and settled down. The list goes on for ever.

Eddie is just one more casualty.

By the age of twenty-two, he had met Sonya, a success-ful dental assistant, and they had decided to marry. Sonya wasn't like Eddie. She was stable and sensible and a bit short on big dreams, frankly. She hated jazz and the trum-pet and was certainly opposed to Eddie making a career out of it. But he loved her and married her all the same.

Once married, stability suddenly became a priority for both of them. They bought a house with a mortgage and a car with a bank loan; they enrolled for pension plans and insurance policies, healthcare payments and investment schemes. Eddie stuck with his job, not because he liked it or was even any good at it, but simply to pay the bills. Sonya stuck at her job too – that is until she became preg-nant with the first of their three children.

That was eighteen years ago.

Eddie never did become a trumpeter, hasn't seen even a fraction of the world, and as for the Rolls-Royce Corniche ... well, as I said, he's a government officer with no promotion prospects, slowly drowning in a sea of debts, and, worse still, his handwriting nowadays looks like this – remember?

He expected that it would meet once

Drab and unthrilling, to put it mildly. What's more, just lately, he's started losing his hair and has taken to wear-ing beige. So where did it all go wrong, Eddie?

He can't tell us, he doesn't know.

As I said before, this story is a bit simplistic, but maybe you've met someone who has made similar choices, found him- or herself stuck in a stifling routine, and who now feels disillusioned and dissatisfied in the same way. It's a common enough plight.

In the words of Boris Pasternak: 'Man is born to live, not to prepare for life.' Yet large numbers of people – maybe even the majority – can't see this. They regularly accept far less than they deserve. Somewhere between the age of seventeen and twenty-five, their ambitions and dreams simply fall apart and, instead, they accept the drudgery of a dull workaday routine, unaware that with a little extra planning, determination and persistence, they could have so much more.

The question is: why should any of us squander the talents and goals that make us unique, simply to be like everyone else? And why, having realized our mistake, do we not do something to remedy the situation?

I mean, if you bought a rail ticket from Paris to Moscow but, quite by accident, climbed aboard a train bound for Rome, would you just sit there meekly and travel all the way to the wrong destination before doing something about it? Of course not. The moment you realized your mistake, you'd leap off and switch trains. Well, life is much the same. Changing from the wrong train – the one marked 'Destination: Despair and Frustration' – to the one bound for 'Personal Fulfilment' is a fairly simple manoeuvre provided it's done soon enough. The longer you leave it, the harder it becomes to leap off.

The conflict here is between the craving for fulfilment which is common to all humans, and the brainwashing we are subjected to as we grow up. If that brainwashing wins the day and we choose not to fight it, our feelings of duality will continue to get worse. If fulfilment wins, on the other hand, and we put ourselves back on the right track in life, our handwriting will take on new vitality and character, and any split t's and l's will start to heal and may eventually disappear altogether.

By way of a footnote to all the above, I ought to stress that we are not scanning a person's handwriting purely for signs of failure and despair. Quite the opposite. By picking out these Telltale signs from the whole and making the writer aware that he is trapped in a cycle of deep-seated frustration, you may be giving him fresh impetus to make positive changes in his world, thereby stimulating him into planning his escape route.

On occasions, life itself has even been known to take a hand in the growth process. Adverse circumstances such as a prolonged illness, the sudden death of a parent, divorce, bankruptcy and so on, may only serve to bring into sharper focus what truly matters in this world and what doesn't. Even something as vague as reaching middle age can be a vital stimulus to action: a person suddenly realizes that the years are ticking by and that he has very little to show for all his effort. This bolt from the blue is often sufficient to give the Duality Victim renewed vigour as well as a reason to escape his comfortable rut and find a more satisfying track.

You'll note, however, that all the examples so far have involved the writer giving in to the demands of a will greater than his own, but what happens when the duality is **self-imposed**, when he makes a deliberate choice to live a lie?

I began this chapter by talking about dating and deception: how so many people adopt an outward persona, one that is different from the way they really are inside, for the sake of making a good impression. They are insecure about some

aspect of themselves: their looks, their personality, or whatever, and so they try to disguise it, wearing a brightly-
coloured mask to deflect attention from the true self behind.

Strictly speaking, this should be listed under the heading
of Duality, but such are the lengths people go to to hide
their weaknesses from the rest of us that I felt it deserved a
section all to itself, and this forms the basis of the third and
final big thing you need to know.

The Third and Final Big Thing You Need to Know

Insecurity

If there is one characteristic for which most of us would swap a kidney, it would not, I think, be beauty, wealth or wit – but supreme inviolable self-confidence.

Matthew Norman

Have you ever stood and watched a herd of dairy cattle mooching around a field, swatting flies with their ears, chewing the cud benignly, and thought to yourself 'Boy, do they have it easy!'?

After all, what do cows do?

They eat, they drink, they produce milk, and, every so often, they give birth to little cows. That's more or less it – the sum total of their life experience.

Not for them the pressures of modern living: no bills to pay, no groceries to buy, no diary heaving with appointments, no pension schemes or mortgages. Not once do they have to fathom out the Japanese instructions in a video manual or learn to operate a power saw. Chronically unfazed by world events, untroubled by fear, never scheming or sly – a cow is just a cow. It does what a cow does and, as far as we can tell, never questions why.

If a cow had handwriting, it would probably look something like this:

Human beings, on the other hand, are different. We have a spectrum of emotions to play with. We can love and hate, we have moods, fears, ambitions, we're capable of great kindness as well as great cruelty; we build, we destroy, we experiment, we suffer and we tie ourselves in knots trying to do the right thing by each other. Our lives are packed with incident. As we grow so we learn, and each lesson becomes embedded in our memory as a foundation for future action.

As children, if we try something new – stick our tongue in an electric-light socket, for example – and it hurts, then we usually avoid doing it again. Conversely, if an activity gave us great pleasure last time around – such as eating ice-cream or jumping in puddles – we do our utmost to repeat the experience as often as possible. In each case, whether we attempt the stunt again is a matter of personal choice. We know the rewards, we understand the consequences, and we decide accordingly whether, say, the pleasure of splashing through puddles is outweighed by the discomfort of squelching all the way home in rain-sodden shoes.

However, life being the crazy roulette wheel that it is, some events happen to us whether we want them to or not – disease, accidents and death being the three most obvious ones. Add to these a whole host of other misfortunes, from the psychological damage caused by cruel, neglectful or overbearing parents, through to excessive feelings of self-consciousness generated by having a stammer or a large facial birthmark, or merely by differing from the norm in some way – an albino, a homosexual, being exceedingly tall or small – and not quite fitting in.

Anyone who has suffered bullying in his early years and felt the terror of relentless persecution must inevitably have a different perspective on the world from that of someone who was left in peace to develop normally. By the same token, how can a woman suffer a vicious rape attack and then carry on afterwards regarding men in a balanced, open way, as though nothing has happened?

Deep and abiding wounds of this nature give rise to great insecurity within the person. Their whole life becomes a balancing act between handling the hurt and letting it out. In fact, going one step further, you could say that, for each and every one of us, our daily life is a challenge in which we juggle the effects of positive and negative experiences we encounter: the praise, the knocks, the successes and the setbacks. And how well we do this is reflected back at us with some precision by our handwriting. Good, expansive responses seem to give the words an overall dynamic thrust, while adversity, if we handle it badly, can inhibit the size and slant severely.

For instance, here is someone who has managed to lay the bad times to rest. Old scores have been settled, past hurts and disappointments were confronted a long time ago and have had their sting removed.

a chance to examine the recipes, and even try them out, it's totally up to you whether you receive any more.

See how the drift is all forward? The underlying energy suggests advancement, striving, an eagerness to move on. No lasting bitter memories here, for sure.

Now, look at this one:

Jan. 9th

Landkerchief, that lovely bottle of scent; how best kind

Notice the difference? The way the **J** and the **t**'s have elongated, ominous tilted cross-bars that reach out across the paper to the left? Again, I know I have not yet explained the meaning of all these signs but, even so, the past trauma shows up well in those streaks which destabilize the letters and act as an anchor, pulling them back. For whatever reason, the writer hasn't been able to release the pain and so it continues to haunt her, colouring her thoughts, preventing her from making proper advances in life and prospering the way she should. Rather than being clear and readable, the page is awash with needless complication. This person is riddled with insecurity; life moves way too fast for her and she is slowly but surely drowning.

Each of us deals with our problems in a different way, though usually we compensate for what we perceive as 'soft spots' by constructing some form of outer shell to conceal and protect them. This is something we all, regardless of intellect or education, do extraordinarily well. Indeed, our shell is often so effective, so subtle, intricate and convincing, that we even come to believe it ourselves.

Recently I was sitting in a café near my home and saw a collision between a young bicycle courier and a

Volkswagen Beetle.

The unfortunate man was pedalling furiously down the road when, without warning, a woman who had just pulled into the kerb opened her car door right in front of him. There was no time to swerve. He sped smack into the door, somersaulted right over the top of it and tumbled away down the road on his back. As you'd expect, the guy was very badly injured, the motorist was in a state of deep shock and, I would guess, neither of their lives will be the same again for a very long while.

There is no doubt that this accident was the motorist's fault and so I guess that, between the two parties and their insurance companies, some figure will eventually be arrived at to compensate the courier for his pain, distress and loss of earnings. Although a lump-sum payment won't repair any lasting damage to his body, it will at least restore some kind of balance to the situation.

If we gash ourselves on a sharp blade, no matter how bad the wound may seem at the time, eventually new skin will grow over it, perhaps leaving a small scar. And much the same thing happens with emotional injuries. A deep emotional wound leaves a scar on the unconscious mind. Framing this in terms of our ocean liner again, everything may appear fine above deck, but when a bad experience hits us and we get holed below the water-line, our brain does some hasty repair work to patch up the mess. If it didn't, the whole ship would go down.

In the case of childhood trauma, we don't look to other people to compensate us for our injury, we do the repairs ourselves. Sometimes we try to remove the sting from the negative emotions by first denying that they hurt us anyway – 'Who – me? Offended? Goodness no. I take that sort of stuff in my stride' – before burying them as far down as they will go in the hope that any bad memories will fade with age, the way an old photograph does. Or else we accept that we *are* hurt, but rather than confronting the pain and dealing with it there and then we soldier on regardless, maintaining a brave face and a stiff upper lip. We deal with the issues as best we can, and **compensate** for the damage with an adjustment to our personality and behaviour patterns.

MAURICE

Maurice is a forty-five-year-old Canadian: highly intelligent, witty, eloquent and quite charming when he wants to be.

He is also short.

Exceedingly short. In fact, by the age of eleven he was still no bigger than a ventriloquist's doll. Not a dwarf or anything, just naturally... compact, like a scale model of a human. Unsurprisingly, and because kids can be so relentlessly cruel, Maurice quickly became a target for pint-sized jokes at his high school. For years he was tormented almost non-stop; bullies called him stupid names, knocked him over, kicked and punched him. On top of this, he was regularly ignored in class and locked out of conversations.

Of course he grew used to the cruelty and the jibes, putting on the requisite brave face throughout, pretending he didn't care, that it was all a bit of a giggle really. He let all the jokes go right over his head – literally – and later on even gave an amusing name to the discrimination against him: 'apart-height', he called it.

But how do you think he really felt inside? Hurt, crushed, afraid, victimized?

You bet. And more besides. Every night, as a child, he must have gone home and wept into his pillow at the injustice of it all, wishing he could grow an extra few inches.

But he didn't, of course – not noticeably anyway.

Eventually, reality set in. He was always going to be shorter than most other people, so he had no choice but to learn to deal with it.

And the way he did deal with it is fascinating.

Maurice decided that what he lacked in physical stature he would make up for in personal presence. For a start, he began to talk louder – that way others were bound to notice him. Further, when they pushed him around, he just stood his ground and pushed them right back. He got angry too, yelled back at the bullies who antagonized him, threw his books aside and tore into them, kicking and screaming. He got more than one black eye this way, but that didn't seem to matter. Unable to contain his fury any longer, he had to fight back.

These days, he spends much of his time as a political campaigner, fighting injustice on behalf of underdogs like himself and doing so with great passion. The anger, it seems, has never really left him. He has a fierce temper, still talks loudly and uses his position and influence to dominate and intimidate. Years later, he continues to vent that old childhood pain on his colleagues and family. Far from coming to terms with the problem, he deals with it in the only way he knows how – by inflicting upon others the anguish he suffered repeatedly as a small frightened boy.

For obvious reasons, I dare not show you a sample of Maurice's handwriting – litigation can be very expensive! – but here is something similar, belonging to a small angry person...

progress again before Thursday

Notice how tight it is, how direct and small, yet in some ways just aching to grow bigger. Once you have read through the Alphabet, return to this sample and check out the venomous **d**'s, the tight spiteful little **e**'s and the furious, fighting **g**'s.

This condition came to be known as the Napoleon Complex (after Napoleon Bonaparte, the brilliant eighteenth-century Corsican general who, due to his pronounced nanostature, developed a quite obnoxious temperament and used it to stunning effect in getting his own way) – and is best summed up as 'the smaller the person, the larger the personality'.

But hang on, there's more.

COLIN

Colin has the opposite problem to Maurice. He is in his early twenties – quite good-looking, bright, amusing, but extraordinarily tall at about 6' 7". By the age of fifteen he already stood an astonishing 5' 10" in his stocking feet, and was naturally very sensitive about the fact.

Of course, kids never made fun of Colin to his face – they wouldn't have dared! Nevertheless he was made acutely aware that his pale lanky frame towered way above everyone else. He suffered constant enquiries of 'How's the weather up there, Lofty?' and the like – nothing too harmful, merely a reminder that he was 'different'.

Although it proved a constant problem, in this instance the condition also brought major advantages – he was a demon at basketball, for instance, and won several high-jump trophies for the school; and he certainly never got pushed around. But oh, what he wouldn't have given to be a foot shorter and blend in with the crowd. His attempts not to stand out included hunching his shoulders into a permanent stoop, developing a really soft voice and an even softer temperament, never speaking out of turn, rarely making his mark in any conversation and staying well in the background.

Even today, Colin hasn't changed much – he is still a gentle giant, big, friendly, shrinking into the crowd, keeping a low profile and seeking anonymity wherever possible. As a consequence his handwriting looks like this:

Hope these arrangements are O.K.

Actually, there are several flaws in the way he writes, as any expert will tell you, but, all the same, it is a quiet, open and unprepossessing hand. No spikes, no venom, just an easy-going character, relaxed with plenty of good humour.

In life, Colin compensates for what he perceives to be his great weakness by behaving in a contrary way. The big difference between him and Maurice is that, in Maurice's case, by taking his stroppy no-nonsense behaviour to such unacceptable extremes, he goes beyond merely compensating for his lack of size, he is *over*compensating for it, and here is where the real problems start.

OVERCOMPENSATION

When we *over*compensate for a problem, we build a set of strong, almost unassailable external defences to protect our wounded, vulnerable interior. But we tend to go too far.

The outer behaviour, whilst intended as a distraction to keep the world at bay, merely betrays the turmoil bubbling away beneath, in much the same way as an ill-fitting toupee, perched like a dead ferret on an old man's head, says to the world, 'Actually, I'm bald under here, you know.' The disguise is so obvious, it simply draws attention to the problem it is intended to conceal.

*   *   *

Example 1: Tina

Tina holds a senior managerial position with a PR company.

While she was growing up, her father was unremittingly cruel to her, beating her, bullying her, withholding meals as punishment, making her young life a living hell with no possibility of relief or escape. For a full fifteen years this authority figure in her life was the focus of her hatred, and in time she came to believe that men everywhere would behave in the same unforgivable way.

As a mature adult, Tina is now a staunch campaigner for justice; she believes in equality and freedom and does all she can to fight sexism, racism, ageism and just about every other ism you can think of. She still recalls her feelings of helplessness, of not being loved or cared for by her father, and compensates for it by appearing almost superhumanly fair in her dealings.

Or at least that is her attitude towards women. For the male of the species she reserves a different tactic altogether.

Unable to prevent the longstanding hatred of her father spilling over into her everyday dealings, and fuelled by thoughts of revenge, she continually seeks power over her male colleagues, feeling she must score points against them, wherever possible undermining their confidence with criticism and unwarranted verbal abuse. Understandably, the men can't work out what they have done wrong, and even she has no real idea how crippling her personal attacks can be.

Unconsciously, Tina is still at war with her father, but because it is a war she can never win, inevitably she will continue to vent her grievance on every man she meets, overcompensating wildly, until the day comes – if it ever does – when such lingering hatred is released and dealt with.

Example 2: Clive

Both of Clive's parents died in a car accident when he was three years old, after which he was raised by an aunt who was generally cold and unfeeling towards him and, at the earliest opportunity, shunted him off to a boarding school notorious for its authoritarian regime.

Home life too was highly disciplined. His aunt reined him in constantly, controlling him, disciplining him and keeping his whole life in check. In the end, desperate for freedom, he became a rebel with a deep loathing of all forms of authority: uncontrollable, anarchic, dropping out of school at the earliest moment, and all the while secretly, unconsciously, pledging that one day revenge would be his.

This outcome is hardly surprising. A child who receives proper amounts of love and attention, who is guarded and guided sensibly through his formative years rather than bullied into following someone else's example, will generally become a confident adult, sure of his own mind and able to receive and give love to others. Children subjected to unyielding authority early on, starved of genuine affection when they need it most, tend to grow up either fearing authority or even fighting it.

At twenty years old, Clive has calmed down considerably and is now at college studying to become a therapist, with a particular emphasis on hypnotherapy. Using various mind-control techniques he hopes one day to treat clients for a range of mental problems and addictions. Although he may not recognize the link, this is Clive's way of turning the tables. Under the guise of counselling he will at long last gain power over other people, controlling their minds and behaviour just as his aunt and teachers did to him all those years ago.

Although Maurice and Colin and others like them, when

they compensate for insecurity caused by longstanding psychological problems, choose the masks they wear with great care, those who *over*compensate are usually unaware of the nature of their disguise. Because it develops more naturally and at a slower pace, they fail to make the connection between the problem itself and the methods they use to deal with it. Try telling Tina that she treats men badly because of the unsatisfactory relationship she had with her father, and she would laugh in your face! To her, men are just not as good as women, and that's that.

Evidence of overcompensation can always be found in the handwriting. Both Tina and Clive draw puffy, balloon-like letters, something along the lines of:

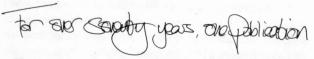

This is a dead giveaway to the masks they are wearing. The puffiness means they use their respective personalities as a buffer and protect themselves by ensuring that they always go on the offensive first. In this way, they can be absolutely certain no-one will ever penetrate their barricades.

INSECURITY

Spotting signs of other people's insecurity can be a fascinating pastime, though maybe not so fascinating when someone is doing it to you – so be warned! The man in the dead-ferret toupee clearly thinks he looks great and doubts that anyone will spot the cover-up, but if the roles were reversed and it was you who were wearing a cheap rug, you wouldn't thank passers-by for pointing it out and giggling, now would you?

Anyway, the material available for study is endless. There

will always be a trace of some kind of insecurity in a person's handwriting for the simple reason that we are all insecure about *something*.

For instance, what else but a feeling of profound insecurity would cause a short fat guy to drive a huge expensive car? Clearly, the car is there to restore balance, compensating for what he feels he lacks in the stature department. As he cruises by majestically in his white Rolls-Royce with the customized number-plate, this chap believes he's making a bold statement: 'Look at me – I'm successful.' When what he is actually saying is: 'I'm not *really* short and fat, you know. Well, OK, I may be a bit on the short side, but I've also got plenty of money, so you can't look down on me any more like you used to when I was a kid.' If he were to quit worrying about what people think of him, quit trying to be something he is not, and just *be himself*, he would be far more contented.

Don't misunderstand me, there is nothing wrong with having wealth. Wealth is great. But to parade the length of the high street in a flash car merely to prove how wealthy you are, is not. You might as well wear a sandwich-board announcing, 'I am insecure!'

It would certainly be cheaper.

Too many of us confuse being wealthy with being rich. A person is rich when he lives a joyful balanced life with a clear understanding of the role he is intended to play during his few years on the planet. If he can give and receive real love in equal measure, has health and freedom, a touch of wisdom and an unquenchable thirst for living, and on top of all that is fulfilling his true purpose, then he is indeed rich. Should he make a lot of money too, that's fine. But don't ever suppose that acquiring vaults full of cash is the same as being rich, because it is not. There are dozens of lonely, depressed millionaires in this world. Money pays the bills, it doesn't buy you riches.

However, as we saw with Tina earlier, insecurity can also be a great motivator. Without it, most of us would be robbed of any incentive to improve our lot in life. Indeed, if we spent even a fraction of the time in achieving our goals that we do in hiding the insecurity which *prevents* us from achieving them, we would all be invincible.

Besides, many of the trappings of insecurity are enormous fun.

Fashion is fun. To look good and feel fit and healthy are all worthwhile pursuits. Flash cars are exhilarating and can do wonders for our self-esteem. Big luxurious houses are spacious, liberating, life-enhancing. The aim is not to stand in judgement, condemning these things outright or depriving people of their security blankets, but to recognize insecure behaviour for what it is and then, more importantly, to relate what we have learned to the person's handwriting.

A particularly telling sign of inner weakness, to my mind, is calligraphic script. Once a person abandons his ordinary style of handwriting in favour of a rigidly structured and ornamental one, like this:

The past few years have been nice

. . . it usually highlights a deep identity problem of some sort. On the one hand, the writer may be genuinely artistic with a good eye for presentation; on the other, he clearly cares what people think of him to the extent that he goes out of his way to garner their approval and respect. In its most extreme form the use of calligraphy is a sign of excessive control, the stifling of free expression, possibly even a lack of self-love. By beefing up his image in such a contrived way, he is asking to be appreciated for what he appears to be rather than what he actually is – and if that ain't insecurity, I don't know what is!

In all cases, what you are looking for is the secret story: the core of someone's personality, how he is compensating as an adult for experiences he encountered when he was young. By examining the **energy** given off by the writing, and looking for signs of **duality** and **insecurity** in the way he forms his words, you can piece together in detail the reasons why he behaves as he does.

Anyway, I think that's more than enough potted psychology for now, don't you? It's time to make a start on the Telltale System itself and learn how to spot all the above traits in a person's handwriting.

Where to Begin

Faced with a fresh piece of handwriting to explore, there are several ways you can go about it.

Some people, for instance, like to start by analysing certain key letters, homing in on a particular character trait which interests them – romance, self-discipline, nosiness, or whatever it may be – and working things through from there; while others tend to single out particular words or phrases and concentrate on those to the exclusion of all else.

For me, the best way to begin is by taking an overall view of the writing. Ignore the words themselves for the time being, forget their meaning, just focus on the *look* of the page and try to catch a whiff of the personality behind it. Ask yourself a few basic questions: how big are the margins? Do the lines of the writing slope upward or downward? Are the individual letters large and flowery or small and compact? Do the words fit neatly together or do they wander erratically all over the paper like an intoxicated snail?

Don't worry that you are new to this. First impressions count for a lot, and nine times out of ten a quick glance at the layout will throw up all sorts of fascinating details.

My family have lived in the north of England for over twenty years, in the city of York – a beautiful Roman fortress town with many of its prime historic landmarks still remarkably well-preserved.

While the narrow winding streets and the vast cathedral and the gateways and walls draw in countless thousands of tourists each year, York also has another special claim to fame: as the home of two gigantic chocolate factories, Rowntree's and Terry's.

Many of the UK's most popular chocolates are made there – Kit-Kats, Yorkies, All Gold, After Eight Mints, the list goes on and on – meaning that on a good day, when the vats are churning and the wind is in the right direction, the whole city becomes engulfed in the thick, powerful aroma of freshly-made chocolate. It can almost knock you off your feet sometimes. Indeed, to many visitors, that fabulous cocoa smell *is* York, and sums up the strengths and attraction of the city far more than any of its visible touristy historical features.

Now, although handwriting may not give off a smell exactly, there is much more to what you see on the page than a few well-chosen words shaped into sentences and punctuated. It has a feel and a spirit to it, a special energy which *is* the writer.

Below, you will find nine Telltale Signs worth looking out for as you go.

1. THE MARGINS

You can tell a lot about a person from the size of his margins.

The Computer Print-out

If the page looks something like this: precise, well-ordered, with the writing boxed in neatly as though laid out by computer, the writer has good self-control, knows his limitations as well as his strengths and plans his work – and probably his life too – down to the last detail. He is strict on himself and others. Having begun something, he always sees it through to a natural conclusion. Security is important: he does not care for too much risk. Further, if the words are well-spaced, the writer takes great care with every task he undertakes and gives a lot of thought to all aspects of his life, never diving in impetuously.

The Gushing Drain

Symptoms: tight, thin little margins all the way round and a blizzard of words. This is someone whose idea of living does not always coincide with other people's – he may see the world from one perspective and be surprised when others fail to fall in with that view. Low on self-control, often over the top, he gives too much of everything. So if he is joyful, that joy is unconfined; if he feels hurt or rejected, he will cry enough tears to fill a small reservoir. If the words are packed together in tapeworm-like sentences, forming one continuous stream of consciousness, he will be intense, probably blind to reason and self-absorbed.

The Drifter

Begins well but ends sloppily. This person launches into projects with the very best of intentions, and then gets sidetracked and loses his way. He takes on a commitment only to regret it almost immediately. Enthusiasm quickly evaporates, concentration lapses. He acts first, thinks later. Plans go awry quite often and goals become fuzzy. The sort of individual who, having pledged to give up smoking for life, will be found a week later pacing up and down outside the tobacconist's with a pained look on his face, rattling his loose change.

The Late Developer

Opposite to the above – begins unsurely but ends well. Slow to commit to anything, though when he finally does so he'll usually honour the agreement. He may be lazy or lacking in enthusiasm or slightly over-cautious at times, but eventually will pull himself together and give the appearance of knowing what he is doing.

Intensity Plus

The perennial clock-watcher, this person lives in fear of being late for appointments and will turn up at least half an hour before the pre-arranged time just to be on the safe side. There is a nervous anxiety here which pushes the writer to panic and fret when things don't run smoothly. Worries needlessly, takes criticism to heart and is constantly arranging, rearranging, checking, and planning and adjusting to ensure a smooth ride. Being calm and relaxed to begin with would achieve much the same aim.

The Crammer

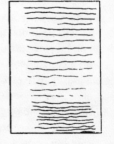

Starts well but is hopeless at planning ahead. If twenty tasks need to be completed by 5 p.m., then six of them will be done to a high standard by 3.30, and the remaining fourteen dashed off in an almighty rush at the last minute, or fobbed off onto somebody else. The sort of person who will hold up an entire aircraft by checking in an hour late without a ticket and with nineteen items of luggage to be stashed in the hold. 'Sorry' is his favourite word. Infuriating.

The Slow Burner

Symptoms: variable margin-size, generous spacing between words. If there is no definite margin, the writer is probably innovative or at the very least unpredictable – the sign of the gentle dabbler who does a bit here, a bit there, but has no consistent game-plan in life. Ridiculously spaced-out words indicate a person who hates to be rushed: too cautious, too thoughtful, too wary. He may plan to go on holiday next summer, but by the time he's read the brochures and decided on somewhere, it's autumn and they're out of date.

2. THE SLOPE

Many people prefer to write their letters on lined paper in order to keep the sentences level and straight and readable. For others, even *with* the aid of lines, their writing still slides all over the place, first one way, then another, as though they have no control over their pen. There is nothing wrong with this, and to be an individual is always preferable to conforming to the way you've been told things should be done. But whichever way the writing slopes it helps us to decide whether the writer has an optimistic temperament or a gloomy defeatist one.

The Optimist

The writer can't prevent his words swinging upward. This is the sign of someone who is essentially content with his lot. He may have upsets and down-times, but whenever the dark clouds roll in he always manages to find a silver lining out there in the gloom. Bear in mind that, if the words creep too steeply up the page, you may be dealing with someone who is blindly unrealistic. Otherwise, this is the best sort of person to have around when you need cheering up.

The Pessimist

Here, gravity itself seems to be dragging each sentence down towards the floor. This person revels in the more serious side of life rather than the upbeat aspects. To his mind, hopes are there to be dashed, projects doomed to fail, people destined to disappoint and deceive. The world is one huge dreary tableau of defeat, death, poverty, misery, famine, hypocrisy, disaster and pain. For some mysterious reason, such people often end up as children's entertainers!

The Reformed Pessimist

A variation on the above. Here, although the lines of writing may not slope upward, individual words or phrases do. This person is fighting off thoughts of failure. He manages it for a while, but then the same evil doubts come back to haunt him. He wants to be successful and win through, but however much he tries he can't make himself believe that everything's fine. Something *must* go wrong, surely! And lo and behold, it always does.

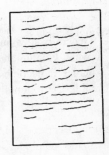

Worried of Wolverhampton

Troubled, confused, at odds with himself and other people, this character can't decide which direction is best. One line drifts upward, the next plunges down; some words are floating, others trip over themselves and collapse in a heap. The writer takes on too many commitments or weighs himself down with worry. A positive thought is cancelled out almost at once by a negative one. Unless he can control his babbling-brook mind and bring some order to his plans and life, he may find that a lot of effort has been put into going precisely nowhere.

3. THE SIZE

No matter what you've heard elsewhere, size *is* important.

Generally speaking, the larger the writing, the more flamboyant, volatile and larger-than-life the writer will be. The smaller it becomes, the more narrow-minded, controlled and less emotionally fulfilled he will tend to be.

So, for example, Father Christmas might write like this:

ho ho ho ho!

On the other hand, that odious little man at the bank who sends you a rude letter if your account so much as tiptoes into the red probably writes like this:

I refer to your letter of 14ᵗʰ February '94 and will arrange to close the account.

Heavily compacted lettering is a sign of suppressed feelings, and belongs to someone very down-to-earth who believes in self-control, prudence and circumspection at all times. Scientists are extremely prone to this, fixated as they are on minor theoretical details rather than the delights of self-expression and wilder living. Feelings get denied, desires bottled up, possibly for ever. As a result, and unless countered at a reasonable age, the writer's life, viewed as a whole, may lack a sense of growth and balance.

Then, of course, there is a blend of the two: gigantic capital letters at the beginning of words followed by much smaller letters for the rest:

My Love London

Somehow this just doesn't look right, does it?

Those enlarged capitals indicate that the woman who wrote this puts on a dazzling display of enthusiasm, proving she has an energetic, outgoing personality. Except that she hasn't – not really. The difference in size proves how superficial the display is. By seeking to impress others in this way she is overcompensating for her insecurity, disguising the fact that, underneath, she is an altogether more meek, studious and uncertain character.

In some instances, the writing shrinks to the size of the bottom line on an optician's eye-chart:

a separation is the only way to relieve what must

Instantly you know that vast amounts of pent-up emotion are trapped inside the person, emotion he feels unable to express. Out of fear, apprehension or shyness, he has withdrawn inside himself and built a secure fortress around his heart. If, by chance, any of this emotion escapes – for instance, when he is criticized and becomes flustered or loses his temper – then it does so in short intense bursts, like cannonfire from the battlements, and continues until he regains control of the situation and withdraws inside the fortress once again.

Conversely, if you should ever happen upon handwriting in which lower-case letters are the same size as upper-case ones, so that it has a vaguely 'Written in Toytown' look to it...

Hope that this is OK

...then you know you are dealing with a Peter Pan character.

He or she is refusing to grow up and sees little reason for doing so. There is a good deal of fun, innocence, openness and – dare I say it? – childishness about the person. This means he will resist becoming overly cynical, negative, pessimistic, argumentative, moody... or any of the other nasty things adults tend to be. Equally, he may also be missing out on many of the pleasures to be gained by maturing naturally.

Bear in mind, the size of your writing can vary from day to day. Much depends on the mood you are in, or the mood of the people you're with, or on what is happening at work or in your marriage, and whether the postman brings a surprise gift in his sack or a huge unexpected tax bill.

All of us have bad times in life – periods when our handwriting seems to lack energy and our pen stumbles across the page like Pinocchio with a hangover. This can go on for weeks and weeks, until one day, out of the blue, something good happens – you win on the horses or receive an inheritance, or the promotion you were so desperate for suddenly comes through. Hey presto! You're happy again and that tired old handwriting bursts back into bloom.

Clearly, external factors such as these must be taken into consideration when making your judgement about a person. Don't leap to conclusions and presume, simply because his handwriting is cramped or confused and unreadable, that he is some kind of basket-case. Ordinary everyday trouble and strife may be at the heart of the problem.

4. THE SLANT

Just as crucial.

Handwriting with a forward slant is the mark of an active, enthusiastic, go-ahead, up-front personality. It may not

always be apparent on the surface, but this character has a
clear plan of action and is going all-out to make it a reality.

*danced into the sky whirling and swirling
and banging - Georgia said they were*

Just feel the energy in that! It positively races across the
page, falling over itself to get its message across and be
understood.

By contrast, a backward-slanting writing is the mark of a
more cautious person. When events threaten to move too
fast, he will resist until he is sure of the right path to take.
On the whole he is usually happier to watch and wait than
up and go.

*Very many thanks
& all good wishes*

Just because the handwriting indicates caution, you must
not assume that the writer is dull or dithery. Indeed, the
above example belongs to a woman with a strong, vibrant
personality. What it does mean, though, is that she prefers
to consider her moves and options carefully before committing herself to them.

Anyway, in all cases, the greater the degree of slant, the
more pronounced these traits will be.

5. ALL THINGS CONSIDERED, IS IT EASY TO READ OR A BIT OF AN UGLY MESS?

By that, I mean the difference between this:

Saturday evening was enjoyable

And, at the other extreme, this:

I shouldn't say anything about my childhood days.
I just thought you might wonder why

The first is legible and very open. The writer injects a natural energy and flow into the words and is therefore easy-going, uncomplicated and sensitive, with a reasonable emotional balance and a positive attitude to life. The second could only have been written by Quasimodo, or at least someone equally disturbed. It lacks form, direction, control, balance, clarity, judgement and vision, from start to finish. Take it from me, messy, disorderly handwriting is either the product of a messy, disorderly mind, or of someone who is so laid-back and indifferent to what is going on around him that he has ceased caring what his handwriting looks like.

To use our ocean-liner analogy again: no matter how clean and tidy and well-ordered things appear to be above deck, if the hull is seriously holed below the water-line, then the ship will still go down. In cases of extreme mental turbulence, where a thousand thoughts are somersaulting through the writer's brain at any one time, and where the unconscious is troubled by lasting pain, then words break up, letters merge with each other until they are unrecognizable, whole lines of words wriggle in every direction as the writer wrestles with his emotions. The written word acts as a prism through which all his feelings are filtered until they reach the page as a jumbled, tangled, unreadable mess.

6. FLOORS AND CEILINGS

Have you ever come across somebody who writes using a ruler for guidance, so that every letter sits evenly on the page, giving the words a curious flat underbelly?

I hope these examples are ok

Something like that.

And have you ever wondered why anyone should bother to employ such a laborious, time-consuming method?

For a start, they think it looks great. They'll tell you: 'I like things to look neat.' But the real reason runs far deeper and lies in a yearning for personal support. By resting on a ruler and bringing so much control to what would otherwise be a free-flowing stream of self-expression, they are revealing their deepest fears of being unloved or starved of affection, even abandoned. In life they grab onto what security they can, all the while expecting it to drop away at any moment, leaving them exposed and vulnerable.

This trait is most common among young teenagers who feel unsettled at home – even when their fears are wholly unfounded. But it needn't stop there; the same fears may percolate through into adult life. The solution, interestingly enough, is not to remove the ruler, that will solve nothing. Rather, it lies in learning to trust others more and daring to take greater risks. Often the writer discovers that allowing oneself to be vulnerable does not automatically invite exploitation in return; that the value of unconditional loving far outweighs any pain suffered along the way, and that a state of confidence and secure independence is only arrived at by having faith in those around us. Eventually, and because therapy works from the inside out, the ruler will just fall away naturally.

Writing which has a ceiling to it and which looks cramped
or crushed...

If extra copies are required they

...is telling you that the person's aspirations are being
kept in check. He longs for escape, to grow, develop and
explore.

Crushed handwriting like this is very common among
schoolgirls as they move through puberty to become young
women. They have attained a certain level of maturity, but
without any of the corresponding freedoms that go with it,
and feel thoroughly frustrated.

Elsewhere, the words have a ceiling when the writer has
done his best to earn promotion and recognition at work,
but has never received the rewards he thinks he deserves.
Maybe he goes some way towards achieving his goals and
expressing his talents and feelings, but at the last minute,
out of fear or lack of confidence or both, stops short and
never really allows himself to make the grade. He feels held
back all the time and probably blames others for his lack of
success, without realizing that, all the while, it is he who is
to blame for this predicament.

As we shall see later on, the letters to look out for here are
double l's, as in:

my pillow is overfilled

See how stunted they are, and how they fail to rise up as
high as they should? In such cases, the message is clear and
simple: 'So far and no further': the writer has reached a
watershed in his career and must either tackle the problem
head-on in his current workplace or consider alternative
avenues for his talents.

7. SHARP OR ROUND

Great Houses of Great Britain and Wales

Lawrence King is giving a wonderful party

Sharp, dynamic handwriting like this belongs to someone who is quick on the uptake, witty and maybe even acid-tongued too, at times. He will be swift in spotting mistakes, not to mention trickery and foul play, and won't suffer fools gladly. You can bet there is never a dull moment when this guy's around.

If the writing was even sharper, the person who wrote it would be rather difficult to deal with. Such people are sure of their views, do not court popularity and will gladly sacrifice it when necessary for the sake of getting things done and making their point. However, if this is true – in other words, the sharper the writing, the blunter the person – then it must follow, logically, that the rounder and bouncier the writing is, the more malleable, sympathetic, warm-hearted, tactful and just plain *nice* the person will be, right?

Wrong.

It may be the case *some*times, but certainly not always. This, for instance...

So useful You are always so clever at finding things.

...belongs to a nice person. Whereas this...

Only our publication has stood out from the crowd.

...doesn't.

Rounded **a**'s and **o**'s are an indication that you are dealing with an open, generous, sensitive individual. But this only applies if the rest of the handwriting backs it up, and even then only if the letters are of a normal size. The moment the letters grow too big and become puffy and exaggerated, niceness generally flies out of the window. Instead, you're dealing with a deeply-wounded individual, someone who, in the past, allowed himself to be used as an emotional archery target, and who has now erected a series of defences against the world so as not to appear too vulnerable and thereby risk getting hurt again in future.

You will recognize this scenario from previous chapters. Remember Tina and her bloated writing? Remember how she bullied all the men around her as revenge against her cruel father?

The defences may take a variety of forms: perhaps the writer comes over as arrogant, tyrannical and bad-tempered, or perhaps he rides roughshod over people without taking their feelings into account. In all cases, the method of concealment merely draws attention to the problem itself.

So if you come across **o**'s the size of watermelons: $\bigcirc$, and **a**'s shaped like oven-ready turkeys: $\bigcirc\!\!\!\frown$, then look not for a warm, glowing, happy-go-lucky character, but a wolf in sheep's clothing.

8. SPLIT STEMS

Stems are the vertical spines to be found in such letters as **t, l, b, h** and **d**. They represent the writer's strength of character, his backbone, and should be straight, strong lines drawn in a single stroke. They should not look like this: δ , or this: ∂ , or this: ∂ , or be riddled with loops, hooks and other fancy adornments.

Above all, they should not be split. If they are: Λ $\mathcal{K}$ and one half of the letter is clearly pulling away from the other, almost tearing it in two, it reveals a tug-of-war going on in the writer's mind. Frustration is generated when he wants to move forward and achieve certain goals only to find his initiative restricted either by current responsibilities or by insecurities rooted in the past.

Once the back of the stem begins peeling away from the front, as it does here: *d*, and, less obviously, here: *c*, it means that the person is experiencing fundamental personality problems, a throwback to times gone by, which still serve as stumbling blocks to his advancement and personal fulfilment even today. One set of values or beliefs pulls him one way, while another set drags him the other.

The more severe the peeling – and this: *t* would be considered pretty severe by anybody's standards – then the worse the confusion has become.

There is no telling how problems of this nature will manifest themselves in daily life: perhaps in long-term marital difficulties, or the writer may have trouble making friends or relating to people, or he may simply feel puzzled about his role or direction in life. In each case, the split stem is the telltale sign to this ongoing battle.

Incidentally, when I say 'vertical' in this context I mean 'upright'. And when I say 'upright' I mean in accordance with the overall slant of the handwriting. If there is a pronounced left or right slant to it, then 'vertical' means that the stem should be parallel to all the other letters. So for our purposes, the **t** in this word is vertical: *bat* even though it's leaning to the left, and so is the **t** here: *goat* even though it's leaning to the right.

Above all, and in every case, remember: *stems should not be split in two.* They ought to be a neat single line every time.

9. LOOPS, KINKS, HOOKS AND STREAKS

Most of us customize our handwriting in some way or another.

We add a loop here, the odd twirl there, or some other decorative trinket to catch the eye; and we do so, firstly, because we get the urge to, and, secondly, because we think it adds a certain character to the writing. To us these additions mean nothing, they just inject a little extra style into the words. However, this is not the case. Every one of these trinkets is significant and highly revealing.

i) Loops, and by that we usually mean this sort of thing: *ℓ* or: *G*, indicate pockets of nervousness, apprehension, fear or inhibition which the writer brings to his everyday dealings. Perhaps he thinks too much about issues, or holds back from taking action or committing himself in certain circumstances for fear of being criticized or attacked.

The bigger the loops, the greater the clouds of self-doubt and uncertainty lurking under the surface.

ii) Kinks aren't much fun either. They reveal dark aberrations in the writer's unconscious mind: concealed distress, feelings of resentment or bitterness towards certain people or organizations, all sorts of deep-seated attitude problems which will jaundice his outlook on the world in general.

Kinked letters have a disjointed rheumatic look about them: *R* .They buckle and twist in all the wrong places: *S* and, in large quantities particularly, point to a very troubled mind indeed – the badge of the perpetual victim, the underdog, a hardened fighter, someone who sees life as a constant battle. Because he holds this view, that's exactly what it becomes.

iii) Hooks can go one of two ways: backward like this: ⌐ or forward like this: ᕫ .
Whenever they point back behind the stem and out across the page, they are clawing at the past; meaning, once again, that experiences, teachings and values from a time gone by still have a tight grip on the writer's mind.

Pronounced hookery can also be put down to regrets, guilt, wasted opportunities, a feeling that the Olden Days were golden days – a sentiment which is usually misguided, if not wholly wrong – and reluctance to live in the here and now and face their troubles squarely and courageously. (For forward hooks see over, p. 68.)

iv) A Streak is simply a line without a hook on the end of it. So instead of looking like this: ⊓ , it in fact stops short and looks like this: ⊓ .
The thought process behind it is the same: it still relates to influences drawn from the past, only this time those old lingering memories have much less of a grip. I mean, you can sit fishing with a line all day, but if it hasn't got a hook on the end of it, you're not going to catch anything, are you? Well, the same principle applies here.

The size of the hook or streak will always be governed by the intensity of the influences. So one this size: R, that is to say short and barely visible, is hardly worth considering at all.

If you still find this influences-from-the-past concept difficult to grasp, try to imagine a signpost... In fact, don't bother, because the illustrator's going to draw one.

Thanks.

Picture the post as the stem of the letter – an **E**, for instance. Any hooks or streaks that venture out to the left of it will almost certainly mean that the past maintains a lasting influence on the person involved: *E* .

By contrast, hooks and streaks reaching out to the **right** mean that the writer has his eyes on what the future may hold:

I'd love to ask Alison as well but have lost her address

Forward hooks and streaks will usually appear only at the end of a line of writing and are easy to spot. Inexplicably, a letter suddenly develops a weird elongated tail that flaps around in the right-hand margin. This will happen many times right the way down the page. Immediately you can tell that the writer is looking to the future, hoping for better times ahead, more recognition, increased attention, more friends or indeed anything else which would add sparkle to the current situation.

agenda

teacher

please

Finally, although I said at the start that there were only nine factors to be on the alert for, please forgive me if I add just one more. A little one.

10. WRITING THAT COMES WITH ITS OWN FANFARE

If a handwriting fair explodes with dozens of copious loops or swirls, if capital **L**'s stretch, pillar-like, up towards the sky, and **t**'s and **H**'s are so elegant and contrived that they have an almost Gothic statuesque quality to them – in other words if it looks something like this:

chronology of the Old Testament severely alone.
Prophets, the Hittites, the neo-Hittites, the Assyrians and

– then the writer will sport a certain volume of affectation in his overall demeanour, you can almost bet on it. Such an individual has a grand, and perhaps even eccentric, approach to life. More than likely he yearns for recognition and praise, often to compensate for feelings of low self-worth. Some people adopt a loud voice, others wear fancy fashion accessories, such as a cape or a monocle, in mundane situations; or else they insist on buying a car that is out-of-date and falling to pieces, but which singles them out from the crowd as it chuffs and wheezes its way along the road at fifteen miles an hour.

CONCLUSION

I realize that a whole stack of rules like this will come as a blow to the more casual reader. There seems to be a helluva lot of theory to learn before you can read between the lines of even the simplest letter or note.

In some ways, it reminds me of a phenomenon which is sweeping the country even as I sit here writing this – a series of bestselling books and posters called the Magic Eye which, from humble beginnings, has mushroomed into a worldwide sensation.

Each picture is stereoscopic and contains a blizzard of computer-generated shapes and colours, most of them quite pretty but, unless you have the key to understanding them, totally meaningless. The trick is to look beyond the patterns into the midst of the picture. Do this for a while and suddenly your brain unscrambles a 3-D image from the blur – of a footballer maybe, or a helicopter or geese in a farmyard, something like that.

It is very clever and has made someone somewhere a huge amount of money.

Well, the Telltale Alphabet is not too different.

Although you probably won't make huge amounts of money from it, and you could stare at a page of writing for ten years or more and still not see a footballer or helicopter behind it, the rewards for understanding the System and then applying it – so that, out of a mass of written words on a page, an overall portrait of the writer emerges – are immense.

So let's now rattle through the Alphabet itself and find out what each individual letter means. First, though, are there any questions?

'Yes. My handwriting seems to change all the time. Some days it's good, other days it's just plain terrible. I probably write in four or five different ways at least. Doesn't that screw up your System?'

Not at all.

None of us writes exactly the same way two days running.

There will be times when everything is going right, you feel really happy, contented and your handwriting flows easily and looks good. But then, maybe only a few hours later, something comes along to shatter your peace of mind – you go down with flu, or receive a shocking piece of news – and immediately your mood takes a nosedive. In next to no time, that confident hand of yours has collapsed into a pathetic heap on the page.

But think back to our ocean liner. A dose of flu or sudden bad news, these are conscious-mind events. They happen above deck, as it were, and only affect you superficially. Because the formation of your handwriting is generated directly by your unconscious mind, the basic shape of it – the underlying telltale details we rely on in the Alphabet – will remain more or less intact no matter what your day has been like. Long-term, if you become wholly stressed out about your problems, then yes, your writing will alter to reflect that, but it's unlikely that even the worst news imaginable would ever stop your engine running completely. Whatever happens, you'll live, and your ship will sail on regardless.

'One last thing: I've been flicking forward in the book, and I've noticed that the Telltale Alphabet isn't in the correct order. The letters are all jumbled up. Surely that makes it very difficult to read?'

You're right, the letters are not in the usual order. But that is only because the Telltale System works by tying particular letters to specific emotions: jealousy, passion, optimism, love and so on.

In examining a piece of handwriting, we take an **r** from here, interpret its secret meaning, take a **G** from over there and interpret that; and then a **b**, or whatever, listing the results as we go. Using these various snippets of information, we aim to build up, piece by piece, a composite portrait of the writer, like a police Photofit.

Every letter can be written in dozens of different ways – a small **f**, for instance, may look like this: $\int$, this: $\int$, this: $\top$, this: $\not\subset$, or this: γ – indeed, there may be four or five variations on that same letter within a single piece of writing. This makes sense if you think about it. After all, each one of us is a bundle of contradictory thoughts and feelings. Sometimes we are in party mood, ready to drink and dance with friends; other times we just want to be left alone at home with a good book and a packet of gypsy creams.

Unwittingly, we plant clues to these varying moods in the words we write. It works rather like the combination lock on a briefcase: only one set of numbers in one particular order will open the case. Get it wrong – even if you're just one number out – and the case stays closed. In handwriting analysis, our job is to gather together all the different aspects to a person's character, to find the right combination that will unlock his personality and throw it wide open. That is what the Telltale System does so well.

I would add that if, while you were flicking through the book, you had carried on beyond the Alphabet to p. 236, you would have found a complete summary chart, putting all the letters in the correct order for easy reference!

Anyway, I think it's time we made a start on the System. In the following pages, the letters are subdivided into five sections:-

i   The Key Letter: **E**
ii   Clues to the character and general disposition of the writer
iii Relationships
iv   Career and business
v   Life generally

Note: For the sake of ease, in all the examples that follow the writer is referred to as 'he'. To do otherwise would cause no end of confusion. Please accept, though, that in each case the rules apply to men and women just the same.

The Telltale Alphabet

The Key Letter: E

> Your starting place when examining a piece of handwriting for the first time is the capital **E**. Incredibly, all the clues to a person's feelings, instincts, thought processes and even sexual capabilities have been packed into the body of this one tiny letter.

If you can't find a capital **E** on the page, it's not the end of the world. The telltale signs included here will usually show up in other places too. But if by luck you do uncover one, then you have a convenient short cut to learning what makes a person tick.

E's have four components: a stem: $/$, and three horizontal lines or bars feeding off it: $\equiv$. Each of these bars corresponds directly to a part of the human body.

As you can see, the top bar relates to how the person thinks, the middle bar to how he feels, and the bottom bar to his interest in sex and the strength of his libido.

Now, immediately I know which one you're interested in. But let's not get ahead of ourselves here. First things first.

THE STEM

As we already know, *stems represent strength of character*, not just in this instance, but right the way through the Alphabet.

So the stem of the capital **E** should always be a confident, firm vertical stroke connecting all three bars together: E. It should not be crumpled like this: E or dishevelled like this: $\llcorner$ or just plain wimpy like this: $\iota\ni$.

Anything that misses the mark suggests that the writer is not as confident on the inside as he appears. Superficially he may seem OK, leading you to believe that he is secure and has his wits about him. But if an E-stem is severely crumpled or lacking in spirit, then there is every chance that the writer will be as well.

Whatever the stem looks like, if it also happens to be much too tall, it signifies big dreams and vast capabilities – and yet, for some reason, the writer short changes himself by settling for much less than he rightfully deserves. In many ways he is cramming a quart of aspiration into a pint pot of reality and feels thwarted at every turn.

*E*ven However, if the *whole* of the **E** is exaggerated and far too big compared to the rest of the writing, the individual concerned is doing the opposite – trying to fill a quart pot of personality with a mere pint's worth of raw materials. He overcompensates for character weaknesses with all sorts of exaggerated behaviour – talking loudly in restaurants perhaps, or wearing eccentric clothes, or riding a penny-farthing bicycle to work – anything to help raise his profile above that of the common herd. Behind the show and the grand theatrical gestures, he's as weak and vulnerable as a new-born lamb.

THE HEAD-LINE

Though not terribly interesting to look at ‾ , *the top bar of the* **E** *is an extremely effective guide to the way a writer thinks*.

E The bar should be firmly drawn and connected to the top of the stem, telling you that the person is strong of mind, intuitive, intelligent and able to grasp ideas very quickly. He finds new concepts and innovations especially stimulating. The shorter and flimsier that head-line becomes, however, the less agile will be his powers of understanding and communication. *Note*: anything too stumpy: *E* and you're probably dealing with Forrest Gump. Go easy on him. Explain everything very slowly, don't make any sudden movements and you should be OK.

E If the top bar is divorced from the stem, the writer is either prone to making impractical suggestions or else is continually proposing plans which he hopes will please other people, but without really thinking them through clearly beforehand.

Once the bar reaches the stage of being suspended freely in mid-air, the person is an out-and-out dreamer – good news if he is just putting the finishing touches to his first science-fiction novel, otherwise any seemingly workable ideas he proposes may turn out to be fanciful and without practical foundation.

THE HEART-LINE

The middle bar of the **E** *represents a person's feelings, intuition and conscience.* If it is sturdy and connects with the stem: the writer is in touch with his emotions. If it doesn't: he's not. That's the rule.

A 'connected' person is usually genuine, honourable, passionate, caring, someone with strong principles who will argue his corner with confidence because he honestly believes in what he is saying. If ever there was a conflict between following his heart and obeying a set of arbitrary rules which he felt to be unjust and wrong, then the heart would win every time.

The shorter the heart-line the weaker these traits become; the longer it gets: , the greater the writer's urge to communicate his feelings to other people.

Once the heart-line breaks free of the stem, it is pretty certain that the writer has lost his way somewhere along the road. Instead of tuning in to his own conscience and feelings, he has become hardened to them and chosen to follow a formula or behaviour pattern or some code of conduct laid down by other people. It may be nothing more than a few social graces or sense of protocol and discipline drummed into him as a child; or perhaps he has adopted certain attitudes by choice, the way a poor person who unexpectedly inherits a castle might affect the airs and graces to go with it.

You would expect a scientist who insists on facts, facts, facts every time, someone who sees emotion or sentimentality as evidence of weakness, to have a disconnected heart-line on his **E**. As would a ruthless businessperson for whom ethics regularly take a back seat to whatever actions will close the deal and make the most money. By the same token, find the chairman of a chemical company whose factory continually pours pollutants into neighbouring rivers, and ask him which is more important: healthy profits or clean waterways. If he replies, 'Er, well clean waterways, of course', then take a look at the heart-line on his capital **E** – fast.

THE SEX-LINE

The bottom bar of the **E** *gauges the strength of the writer's sexual appetite.* A firm, well-drawn bar: E, is the sign of a healthy libido. Indeed, where men are concerned, if the sex-line is strong and slopes upwards provocatively: E, the writer will more often than not be utterly insatiable and constantly on the lookout for his next partner with his tongue hanging out!

Anything shorter – this: E or this: E – may signify:
a) a dwindling interest in the subject;
b) persistent lack of opportunity, or
c) possible organ malfunction!

The sex-line is almost always connected to the base of the stem. When it isn't: E, this is usually a worrying sign. The writer is apt to use sex as a means to an end, treating it as a pleasurable bodily function rather than as a deeply fulfilling spiritual experience. He may not fall under the heading of 'promiscuous', but will probably prefer the one-night stand or odd fling here and there to a committed long-term involvement.

A sex-line which is buckled signals inhibition and often belongs to someone who is either unsure of his or her sexuality or, more likely, unsure how to put it to best use. The greater the buckling, the more pronounced the inhibition.

Sex is dealt with in much greater detail later on, so I'm going to leave it at that for now. When tackling this thorny subject, though, you must also take into account information offered by other letters in the Alphabet, notably **L**'s (inhibition) and **V**'s (performance between the sheets).

So there you have your **E**.

By taking all four components, as described above, you can start putting together a very basic image of how the individual functions, which can then be built upon, a piece at a time, as you work your way through the rest of the Alphabet.

Other **E***'s to look out for*

I don't want to perplex you with a myriad variations on the capital **E**. Listed below you will find a few of the most common ones. If yours is not among them, don't worry. Apply the rules anyway, taking the stem and each of the three bars separately, and you should still be able to make it work.

(Toasting fork) Denotes a certain flexibility of thought and feeling, a willingness to indulge in communication of ideas and emotions at the expense of security and stability.

(TV aerial) Many problems. Tense, intense; brings a bundle of past regret, bitterness, anger to bear on current problems. Life is often quite a strain for someone like this.

(Looped head-line pulling it back) Thinks too much, over-cautious; has to consider every aspect of a situation before acting. Hesitates often.

(Eager E) Leaning forward, desperate to get moving – the mark of an impatient person who wants to see, find out, do, achieve, complete, or whatever, without delay. Champing at the bit.

(Loop behind base of stem at sex-line) Has a lot of apprehension surrounding sex. The cause is usually to be found in the person's upbringing. Maybe he is shy or has been taught that sex is dirty. Certainly, this individual is not relaxed in sexual encounters.

(Streaked head-line) The writer, due to events or experiences in years gone by, brings many preconceptions and fears to present situations. This **E** has a clenched inward-looking feel to it which signifies a closed, intense mind.

(Head-line and heart-line connected) This person draws on his emotional reserves and uses them to endorse and increase his intellectual abilities. His thoughts and feelings are very much intertwined, so he may be hot-headed, or at the very least quite forceful and driven in his approach to life.

(Reverse figure 3) Known as the Showbiz **E**, this belongs to a person with an upfront personality, who is used to being on show and shining brightly on demand.

CHARACTER AND GENERAL DISPOSITION

Strength of Character

I

> **I** stands for Independence. A strong **I** combines a
> solid ego, lashings of self-esteem, courage, confidence
> and a real sense of purpose.

THE COURAGEOUS I

To the casual bystander, something as insignificant as
this: $/$ seems like nothing more than a simple downward
stroke of the pen. But, believe me, a lot of unconscious
effort has been packed into that little fella.

After all, a capital **I** is a stem pure and simple, so by drawing it boldly the writer is saying, 'Sure, I know myself
pretty well. I've got a firm fix on my world right now,
though not such an iron grip that I shy away from fresh
experiences and personal growth. I have many happy memories of times gone by, and I'm stable, mature, strong-

minded and just about ready for anything that life may
throw at me.'

This person's independent nature is emphasized even
more when the words are well-spaced across the page, and
when the **I** is holding its own, standing slightly apart from
the rest of them:

| believe | can do anything

That is how Superman would draw his **I**!

If the **I** grows too big and starts to dominate the
writing, then you're probably dealing with an
egotist, someone with a very high opinion of his
own abilities and an unwillingness to listen to the
views of others.

Too small, and the opposite applies – the writer
is unsure of himself. He may have plenty to offer
the world, but he doesn't offer it confidently
enough and so may miss out on vital opportunities for advancement in life.

THE CLOSED I

Many people draw their **I**'s like this, which is
OK and nothing to be ashamed of, but nowhere
near as positive as the Courageous I above. The
two cross-bars, top and bottom, are a sign of self-limitation.
They tell you that, in many respects, the writer is a creature
of habit. He has a regime and likes to stick to it. And the
bigger those cross-bars become: the more pronounced this trait will be.

Provided there is a good deal of strength left in the stem,
the individual will still be strong and know his own mind –

yet somewhere down the line and for whatever reason, he has limited his horizons. He fears rapid change and is telling you, 'My ideas about life and myself are fixed right now, and unlikely to alter much in the near future.' It is as if his ego and his imagination have had their wings clipped.

Clark Kent would have an **I** like that.

THE BUCKLED I

I in certain instances can stand for Insecurity too.

If you accept that a sturdy **I** embodies strength, stability and a firm backbone, then you must also accept that something as weak as this: (, or this: ꝺ, with its convulsed, backward-curling stem, is not the sign of a healthy, thrusting personality.

People with crippled **I**'s have had a hard time of things. Maybe their marriage went sour on them, or they have suffered more than their fair share of illness over the years. Or perhaps they just see themselves as unlucky or as one of life's victims. Either way, their unconscious mind is buzzing with unresolved conflict and yet they may be completely unaware of how much damage these lingering memories are doing to their confidence.

On one level they may even derive comfort from their discomfort, preferring to sit around with friends endlessly bemoaning their lot rather than daring to confront the root cause of the trouble and maybe succeed in wiping the slate clean once and for all. At the other extreme they may decide to turn their back on the past and deny that anything is wrong, by putting on a sunny disguise that says to the world, 'Don't worry about me, I'm fine.' That way – by denying the truth – they can keep their troubles at bay, or so they believe.

If the writer has a buckled **I**: (, or a backward-looping **I**: ℑ , then no matter how much he tries to hide it with a smile, deep down he is probably aching with negative emotions which need bringing to the surface and releasing for ever.

Insecurity Man and Inner-Turmoil Woman to the Rescue!

Other **I**'s to look out for

ρ   **(Looped)** The writer is cautious rather than bold, considering options carefully before putting ideas into action.

I̲̲   **(Backward sloping with overlong bottom cross-bar)** A person who has limited any possibility of personal development and is also somewhat slow to take responsibility.

I   **(Tall I with short cross-bars)** Immature. Not too set in his ways yet, but lacking a certain breadth of vision and understanding about what life has to offer.

$\overline{\mathsf{I}}$ **(Disconnected cross-bars)** There is still room for flexibility. Behaviour patterns are not so ingrained that they can't be changed.

$\underline{\mathsf{I}}$ **(Top cross-bar disconnected)** This belongs to someone who has learned to be rather selective about the kind of experiences he lets into his world, but he is not completely closed-minded yet.

$\underline{\mathsf{T}}$ **(Bottom cross-bar disconnected)** The writer may have a deep desire to grow and explore different avenues, but current pressures, responsibilities or environment frustrate his efforts and keep him where he is.

Mental Balance

T

> When it comes to assessing a person's sanity,
> whether he is in control, aware, fair-minded and free of
> the influence of any disturbing events in his past, there is
> nothing to beat a capital **T**.

In an ideal world, all capital **T**'s would look like this:
T .

It's everything you could hope for: a strong, upright stem;
level, horizontal cross-bar pivoting lightly on the top. Not
crazy or irrational, erratic or unstable. Just calm, controlled
and perfect. A **T** of that sort belongs to someone of considerable presence who is able to evaluate many different
aspects of a problem and make considered and sensible proposals for solving it.

All the rules about stems apply here too. But most of the
information we need can be gleaned from the cross-bar,
which should be perched evenly on the stem.

THE LEVEL CROSS-BAR

T If the cross-bar is well-balanced on a strong stem, you know that all is well. The writer's outlook on the world is fine, he is of sound mind, with a reserve of practical ideas and sound judgements. Generally speaking his life is ticking over nicely.

The T-bar should always touch the stem. If it is hovering at some distance above, there is a gap between what the person knows intuitively to be true and what he would like the truth to be. His ideas might be somewhat fanciful on occasions – and this tends to be so when the cross-bar is particularly high: ı – yet he may push them through regardless.

A hovering cross-bar person is your typical Bathtime Hero – a legend in his own ... opinion. Either he thinks great thoughts which seldom or never get put into action, or else he conceives plans that are so thoroughly unworkable in practice that they have to be forced through and somehow *made* to work.

THE SEE-SAW CROSS-BAR

There is an all-purpose question to ask when analysing handwriting. It sounds daft at first, but it works every time.

> *'If you built it out of wood, would it still stand up?'*

The perfect capital **T** is so well-balanced that, if you constructed something similar from two planks of wood – one vertical, one horizontal – and stuck it in the ground, it would almost certainly stand up on its own. This is how it should be. Not so distorted or irregular that, if you built one in your back garden, its centre of gravity would cause it to topple over into a flower-bed.

This applies to a whole range of other letters too, including **G**'s, **D**'s and **S**'s. Each of them should have a certain balance and stability within the writing, so that if you were to make a large-scale version for real, they would stand up of their own accord.

If the cross-bar slopes downward to the left, then the writer pays too much heed to experiences or influences in the past. Maybe he learned a difficult lesson and, having got hurt, does not want to go through the same experience again. Maybe he was just brought up to be more cautious than is strictly necessary. These thoughts cloud his vision slightly, holding him back from positive action and possibly preventing him from making rational judgements on a whole range of issues.

If it slopes the other way, he is secretly afraid of what the future holds and will be averse to taking risks or accepting new ideas, just in case he makes an unsound move and fails. He will not accept criticism or suggestions too easily, and will be somewhat over-protective of his opinions, however blinkered they may appear to be to those around him.

The greater the tilt in each case, the more pronounced these traits will be.

Other T's to look out for

(Small T) Narrow-minded and lacks faith in self; needs to expand area of operations, take greater risks and discover what challenges life really has to offer.

(Warped cross-bar) Certain responsibilities have become a crushing immovable burden. Plans and hopes are constantly frustrated; may feel victimized and that he is the carrier of unjust obligations.

(Propeller cross-bar) Confused about what course to take in future; impeded by lessons learned in the past. There is no going backward or forward; spiralling mental turmoil.

(High floating cross-bar over to the left) Prefers to keep the past separate; protects childhood and keeps memories sacred. May be disappointed by life as an adult.

(Reversed and remote) May indicate introversion or a turning-away by the writer from the world. Certainly there is a shyness here, an indication that he is keeping particular information or aspects of his personality secret.

Self-Confidence

D

A capital **D** indicates three things: the strength of a person's confidence, the way he relates to other people, and how diplomatic he can be.

D's should be modest in size in relation to the rest of the handwriting: neither too small, nor so grossly overblown that they intimidate the letters on either side of them.

The stem should be vertical and un-wavering, like the mast of a yacht, and the chest – the curved part – should be perfectly proportioned and affixed to the mast like a sail. No tricks, no embellishments, no complications...

A straightforward **D**, one that is full and rounded with no unnecessary loops on it, will be written by a straightforward person: someone relatively self-assured, never too loud or aggressive, who always tries to be diplomatic and sensitive to the needs of those around him.

Not surprisingly, in the modern world, few people, other than perhaps small innocent children and a handful of nuns, draw perfect **D**'s. Usually, we opt for one of four kinds:

THE TIMID D

Here, the stem of the **D** is fairly strong but the chest lacks body. It may be slightly shrunken, or floppy, or, in the most extreme cases, wedged in so tightly against the stem as to be virtually non-existent:).

Anyone who draws a timid **D** tends to shy away from life's challenges. He may well be blessed with many fine qualities, but at the same time be cursed with an inability to convey their existence to others with any degree of assurance.

There is certainly a lack of charisma here, as well as low vitality when it comes to communicating with others. Perhaps the writer is unnaturally shy and hides his light under a bushel or, instead of squaring up to people and arguing his corner, takes whatever is thrown at him without a fight.

THE SWOLLEN D

In this case, the **D** has a slight bulge to it.

Find one of these in the handwriting and you know that the person has lots of ideas and opinions together with a greater-than-average desire to communicate them.

If he also slices across the middle of his **D**, joining it to the next letter with a long slash, then you're dealing with someone who knows what he wants and is not afraid to seek it out directly. He frequently gets the results he desires.

THE OVERBLOWN D

If the body of the **D** becomes really pregnant, so that it starts to overshadow or impose itself on other letters in the word, the writer is bound to be somewhat demanding and aggressive in his approach. Indeed the more swollen it becomes, the greater will be that person's need to score points, to win battles, to have what he's saying accepted unquestioningly by colleagues and friends. On the positive side, if this person happens to be in charge of a busy office where difficult decisions need to be made almost hourly, then a talent for knowing his own mind and giving firm directions to others will be a godsend.

The key to all Swollen and Overblown **D** cases lies in the stem. Ask yourself: how big is it in relation to the chest?

Is it firm and strong? If so, the writer is probably a good leader who knows his own mind and, despite appearing overbearing at times, is doing his best to express genuine feelings and opinions.

Or is it tiny and almost non-existent? In this case the persona you see on the outside is somewhat misleading. Inside, the individual is deeply insecure and overcompensating for it by putting on a grand performance. This is doubtless somebody who dishes out the dirt but can't take it. He will criticize you openly for your failings, but will be appalled and become *outrageously* defensive if you try pointing his failings out to him.

D-SHARP AND D-FLAT

Some people seem to have the knack, don't they, of saying the right thing at the right time. It's effortless. They always manage to be diplomatic and sensitive to others' feelings, they never impose or offend, seldom irritate or annoy, and are consummate experts at knowing when to speak up and when to remain quietly in the background and keep their own counsel.

Then there are others – and I count myself among them – who, the moment they open their mouth, put their foot right in it.

I've met many extreme examples of this in my time, and I'm sure you have too. People who either ride roughshod over the folk around them, or else try their best to be tactful, only to find that the wrong words spill out uncontrollably at the last minute and upset everybody within earshot. They simply can't help it.

The first character, the diplomatic one, we call **D**-Flat. He has a balanced, rounded look to him, rather like this:

D If you should come across one of these in someone's handwriting, then you're dealing with a moderately self-confident person – and it's usually a woman, I have to say – who is sensitive to people's feelings. She acts in sympathy with those around her and communicates comfortably without making others seethe or tear their hair out. She won't interfere unduly in affairs that don't concern her, or fuss or make a scene in a crisis. Indeed, like Tommy Steele, she'll just do her best and leave the rest to fortuosity!

The second character, the extraordinarily pushy and irritating one, is known as **D**-Sharp.

D-Sharp people tend to be instigators, innovators and achievers. They are direct and determined, and able to drive themselves and others to undertake tasks, however daunting or unsavoury they may be, and see them through to fruition. The downside is that, since they are often so highly charged, such people quickly become frustrated when faced with opposition – especially when it's from dull, apathetic types who simply haven't grasped the problem at all.

This kind of bullish attitude can lead to Big Conflict but, true to type, **D**-Sharp's view will usually be: 'Hey, so much the better'. He enjoys stirring and destabilizing. Enjoys it a lot. To him it's a sign that events are moving along at last, that people are getting off their hairy backsides and striving for fresh targets. It's all grist to the mill as far as he's concerned. And if there's a bit of aggro along the way, well... it's in aid of a good cause, isn't it?

All in all, **D**-Sharp is a bit of a 'character'.

A word of warning: once you come across a **D**-Sharp, don't go jumping to conclusions too quickly. Be sure to search the rest of the handwriting for confirmation of a lively temperament. Do the words seem exceedingly sharp and energetic? Do they look like the read-out from a seismograph? If so, watch out – **D**-Sharp is about!

Other **D**'s to look out for

(**Flattened chest with bottom loop**) Diplomatic, but eager also to relate to others and interact wherever possible. May be motivated by a fear of being alone and so actively reaches out to the world as a means of compensating.

(Sharp chest, small stem) A person with presence, but he is making up for insecurities by being slightly overbearing in personality.

(Tiny stem, huge backward-sweeping chest) This person is easily shocked and is keeping the world at bay. Fears any attack on his beliefs or even actual physical harm.

(Forward-sloping with loops) May be obsessive and compulsive; someone who keeps moving as a means of running away from the past. May seem lively and fun, but at the centre of the whirlwind is a frightened individual who needs to slow down and face up to whatever he is fleeing from.

(Backward-sweeping loops) Thinks too much; may try to cover every eventuality and could appear scheming. Without enough planning, this person hesitates and feels unprepared.

(Raised chest that overshadows following letters) Tendency to override others (possibly innocently) in an effort to move towards important goals. Things which have to be said and done tend to be said and done without reference to the effect they will have.

Humour

e

A little **e** reveals whether a person is cheerful and chatty
and, if so, whether that sunny disposition of theirs
is genuine or just for show.

Every so often you come across people who simply exude
happiness. They greet everyone they meet with a warm
smile and a hug. They ask how you're doing, suggest lunch
dates, press drinks into your hand as they compliment your
clothes and chuckle at your jokes. They seem to have not a
care in the world, but you should never take this at face
value. It may be genuine, but equally it may just be an act,
a contrivance designed to conceal a more serious character
underneath.

An **e** will tell you all you need to know.

THE SMILING e

The perfect little **e** has an impish quality to it, with an eye
and an open mouth, and sits on the page smiling sweetly.

e Just look how much personality is packed into this little chap. He positively sparkles with good-natured fun, don't you think? The way a proper **e** should. Instantly you know that the writer is a cheery person, pleasant and excellent company – which is useful information, especially if you're considering some kind of romantic involvement, or if you are about to interview applicants for a job and want the successful candidate to blend in with the rest of the office.

THE ENLARGED e

e The more confident and smiley the **e** is, the more gregarious and upbeat the writer will tend to be. Such a person will mix well, laugh a lot, expound on a range of subjects with great enthusiasm and wit and generally be a good egg all round.

e Should the **e** grow too big it can become rather dangerous. Chances are the writer has adopted this cheerful personality as part of the mask he wears. It is intended as a decoy, a defence against personal attack and should be taken with a pinch of salt.

THE SHREWD e

e When the eye becomes rather small and tight with an extended sticking-out chin, you are dealing with another person who may not be as amiable as he first appears. Sure, he seems outgoing enough to begin with – full of laughter and pranks and even warm and highly attractive. But take my word for it, it is probably just a front – a display of personality hiding a much shrewder, more serious, conscientious and reserved nature underneath.

An extremely tight eye is a sign of smouldering ambition. The rest of the face may crease into a broad smile (what the playwright Dennis Potter called 'a smile by mouth alone') but take a closer look and you'll see that the eyes remain perfectly serious.

It is probably no coincidence that the small **e** has an eye – since eyes are said to be a window on the soul and, as such, are a dead giveaway to how a person feels inside. For instance, if you are depressed or having a tough day, it is hard to disguise the fact. You may crease your face into a broad smile and go through the motions, but the right energy will not be there. Others will sense your mood. If your eyes express gloom or despondency, people are not going to be taken in by a makeshift grin.

Over the years I have met a number of prominent politicians with shrewd, unsmiling eyes. And TV celebrities too. It's also quite common among businessmen and high-powered officials – anybody, in fact, who lusts after power and/or money, and who will do just about anything to get it, but at the same time is afraid that their naked ambition will be exposed long before they reach their goal.

THE CHATTY e

The chatty **e** stands out from the crowd because of its shape: a pair of jaws with an extended tongue wriggling out from between them. This person is a communicator, someone who has an opinion on just about everyone and everything and is always on standby with a ready reply or a sharp retort. He blends a vibrant personality with a fervent desire to put across a message of some kind or to convince others by the strength and clarity of his argument that he is right. Witty when he wants to be, he speaks as he finds and likes to have the last word – always!

Only if the chatty **e** becomes too small should you be on your guard. This person takes the best of the above traits and condenses them into sharper, more controlled little bursts. He can be deeply unpleasant when roused and packs a venomous punch in any argument.

Generally, although chatty **e** people may not exactly talk in whispers, their vibrant, up-and-at-'em personality disguises a gentler, more insecure individual lurking in the shadows. Treat them with care – they mean no harm.

Other **e**'s to look out for

(Little eye, extended jaw) The sign of a brave face; someone who has high hopes for good times ahead even though such optimism may be unfounded. Says things are going well when he knows they are not.

(Scrappy and inconclusive) Not a confident personality. However 'together' he may appear in public, he is not at all sure of who he is or what he has to offer. Possibly moody, probably immature.

(Upward-stretching with tight jaw) Easily offended. The sort of person who has a nervous laugh and a fear of being ridiculed or embarrassed.

(Over-large eye, small chin tucked under) Appears bright and friendly, but has other motives. Be careful – he's probably up to something!

Anxiety

A

> The capital **A** shows how stressed you are inside.
> You may appear calm and cool, but if your mind's
> in a constant whirl and you find yourself uptight about
> life in general, the **A** is sure to give you away.

The clue to stress lies in the horizontal cross-bar of the **A**.
The closer it is to the tip of the letter, the more anxiety-ridden the writer is likely to be inside.

In a nutshell: A = relaxed person
A = tense person.

A copy-book **A**, one which is well-proportioned like a stepladder, denotes a firm, sturdy and dependable character, someone who strikes the right balance between dealing with the pressures of living and being able to relax completely. Alas, he may also turn out to be slightly immature emotionally. An **A** without frills conjures up the spectre of a life without depth of personality. Great fun but possibly shallow with it.

A If the **A** has a sharp point to it, this is an indication that the person needs to relax more and take pressing problems less seriously. He is tense and alert and this should give his daily dealings that vital edge. He will certainly be no fool.

A The more rounded or flabby it is, the more easygoing the writer will be. Certain matters seem less pressing and can be tackled in a more casual fashion. An untidy desk, unwashed dishes in the sink, what does it matter? They'll be taken care of eventually.

A An **A** that has collapsed in on itself indicates a life lived under great pressure. The writer may be enjoying every challenge that comes his way but he needs to strive for greater balance by setting off the demands of his work against the benefits of rest, repose and exercise.

AN ALTERNATIVE A

In some instances you'll come across a capital **A** that is not the usual stepladder-shape at all. Instead the writer has taken a small **a** and inflated it to four times its normal size. Later on, we'll see how small **a**'s relate to fortitude and the resilience a person shows in the face of life's little crises. Well, when a small **a** is enlarged and used in place of a capital **A**...

Also enclosed a sketch — jobs to give you some idea

...it tells you that certain events in the past still have a significant bearing on a person's thoughts and attitudes today. It may amount to a total fascination with all things historical. Equally, it may be that the writer is unable to throw off a set of particularly troublesome memories that linger on from many years ago, and is having to put on a brave face to hide the pain. Or, at the other extreme, maybe he just prefers to escape current problems by retreating into the comfort of a bygone age.

For some, the Olden Days carry a profound and irrational allure. Their memories of times long gone are cocooned in a warm, reassuring glow, presumably because nowadays events seem to be unfolding at an ever-quickening pace. To them, progress equals danger and uncertainty, whereas incidents etched into history, since they are over and done with, pose no threat at all. All of this is built in to the enlarged **a**.

Other **A**'s to look out for

 (**Triangular**) Relaxed and determined to remain calm and composed in his own little bubble; will not let the outside world upset his plans.

 (**Legs bent**) The burden of life's responsibilities is beginning to take its toll.

 (**Legs splayed out**) Ditto. The writer needs to take stock of who he is and how far down the road he has come. Maybe growth and progress can now only be achieved by relieving himself of any long-term emotional baggage. Time to reassess old attitudes and viewpoints and make a fresh start.

(**Cross-bar connected to leg**) Pockets of calm inside a busy exterior. This person may look fiendishly frantic, but he can also relax when he has to and knows not to let things get on top of him.

Anger

g

> A small **g** tells us how angry a person feels about the way life has treated him. More specifically, it relates to the *cause* of that anger, and more specifically still, to long-term anger generated by incidents in the past.

Earlier, in the chapter on duality, we saw how certain distressing events – such as a harrowing divorce, the death of a parent or loved one, bitterness caused by losing one's job suddenly and without recompense – can throw up unpleasant memories in abundance for many years afterwards.

We may endeavour to subdue such feelings and pack them off to the back of our mind, but it makes no difference. As long as the source of guilt, bitterness or regret remains with us, the anger can never find its true release. The negative charge attached to it may fade a little over the years, but try as we might to forgive and forget, the same old unresolved questions keep on rumbling round and around in our unconscious: 'Where did it all go wrong?', 'Was I really to blame?', 'Could I have done more?'

In the choppy waters of life, residual anger is nothing

more than excess ballast that should have been slung over-
board long ago, and every time you draw a small **g** it is
reminding you of these pent-up thoughts
and feelings which still cast a shadow
over your outlook and which need
clearing out before real progress can
be made.

There are so many possible
variations here that I can't deal
with them all. But let me try and out-
line the main ones for you with a little story.

Have I mentioned my latest novel yet?

It's called *The Sobbing Heart* and is sure to be next summer's Number One Blockbuster.

The plot revolves around the Grouch family, a dynasty of
scheming, no-good cattle-ranchers in turn-of-the-century
Wyoming. United by greed and reunited by their attorney
after thirty years, the seven Grouch sisters – each with a bitter, tragic story to tell – jostle for a place in the will of their
ailing mother.

But who will get the loot?

Read on.

Opening scene: The **Sisters g** are sitting around a large
table in the dining-room of their farmstead, Grouchfork.

Furious g has a puffy face and a curled-around
serpent's tail. As a child she was abused regularly by her father and, try as she might to put the
anguish and hate behind her, she can't. Some years ago she
went through a messy divorce, filled with recrimination.
She cannot forgive her father for beating her, or her ex-hus-
band for cheating on her and, although it may not be obvi-

ous on the surface, this person is racked with concealed bitterness. She tends to be argumentative and becomes angry over minor issues, often quite unexpectedly.

g **Blame-Me g** has a tail too, but it swings around into a sort of finger, pointing in at itself accusingly. Until five years ago, she had a blissful family life. Then one day, following a violent argument, her only son killed himself tragically, leaving a suicide note that placed the responsibility for his death squarely on her shoulders. She still spends many hours wrestling with her conscience, refusing to carry the can. 'Am I really to blame for what happened?' 'Why is it always me who ends up hurt?' 'Why can't *he* take his share of responsibility?'

Whatever the situation, she is guaranteed always to emerge as both victim and martyr.

g **Forgiving g** has had an easier life. She doesn't remember many bad times in her childhood. Any that there were have been dealt with maturely, and so her tail is more relaxed. Not everything about the past makes sense to her. For instance, she never could understand why her first husband abandoned her to go and live with that rather fey young gentleman he met in a New York sauna. Still, she reasons, there's no point in crying over spilt milk.

Despite the occasional stirrings of resentment, she has a healthy philosophy of letting bygones be bygones.

g f **Relaxed g,** and her twin sister, **The-Past-Is-Over g** are fascinating in that neither of them has a tail at all. Some say they are rather immature and slow to acknowledge any emotional problems, others say the girls are thick-skinned and insensitive. Either way, **Relaxed g**: *g* refuses to carry her troubles around with her and tends to be relaxed in the face of hardship, while **The-Past-Is-Over g** has done an about-face – $\mathcal{P}$ – sweeping any hurt she may feel under the carpet of experience. For her, it's the future that matters. If life throws you a lemon, you make lemonade – that's her motto. Simply dust yourself down and carry on.

Suppression g has a loop dangling down, and this loop varies in size. Some days it's tiny, like this: $\mathcal{G}$ and other days it can be as large as this: $\mathcal{G}$, or larger. It all depends on her mood. Nobody is really sure what she is hiding, though it is obviously some sort of painful memory. All that we *do* know is that, if she is angry, she doesn't show it much. When the loop of her tail is small – $\mathcal{G}$ – the anger is well-buried; when the loop is larger – $\mathcal{g}$ – the memories come flooding back and she becomes more emotional. Whatever the circumstances, and however angry she gets, she prefers to nurse any pain privately or share it with close friends rather than risk ridicule by putting it on public display.

Last of all we have **Defiant g**, a hard-faced young woman whose tail is tucked right in under her head, giving her a kind of fierce grin. She has picked over the past and hardened herself against it. Her schooldays were marred by excessive bullying, and even now she still wrestles with the injustice of it all. These days she settles old scores, not on the people who deserve it, but on her colleagues at work, outwitting them, cheating them, trying to discredit them in the eyes of the boss – whatever it takes to make them suffer, just as she suffered as a child.

Bullying is just one cause. It may even be in someone's nature to be grimly defiant. But however it manifests itself the anger is still in there festering away, and will erupt fairly readily given half a chance.

And there you have it. A mixed bunch, I'm sure you'd agree. The message is simple, though: different people handle their anger in different ways, and the method they use is shown by the size of the tail. The way it hangs – whether it stabs the air: *g* or swings over its own shoulder into a loop: *g* – is your telltale sign to the amount of pain involved and how the writer is coping with it.

Oh, and in case you're wondering what happens to the grasping Grouch sisters: in a neat plot twist, Ma Grouch is revealed to have a rogue illegitimate son called Cecil G who turns up in the next-to-last chapter, and she leaves her entire fortune to him.

Coming soon: *The Sobbing Heart*.

Don't miss it!

Other g's to look out for

(Long, sweeping tail but tight little head) Gets angry spontaneously in response to adverse events, but does not allow himself to become bitter. Once it is over, it is over.

(Elongated S-shape) A person who confuses the cause of the anger with the resolution of the problem. Mixed-up, may feel hurt and bear grudges. Anger has no fixed point, it just simmers underneath.

(Figure 8-shape) Again, anger stewing under the surface is kept at bay for as long as possible until the writer can contain it no longer and explodes.

(Tail bubbles up under the previous letters)
This person is angry with many things and many
people and this lingers constantly beneath the
surface, lending a certain edge and intensity to
the writer's attitude.

Temper

d

In the Telltale Alphabet, the clues to a person's temper –
whether he has one and, if he does, how it manifests
itself – are packed into the little **d**.

What would I have to do to make you lose your cool? Pinch
your parking space? Spill gravy down your best jacket?
Make disparaging remarks about your children? What?

And more to the point, when you do lose it, how does your
anger spill out?

In some cases, a flippant off-the-cuff remark made at the
wrong time in the wrong tone of voice is enough to trigger
an explosion and unleash streams of abuse. While other
folk, somewhat less expressive, are content to seethe. They
may sulk a bit or go quiet, or throw up their hands with a
deep sigh of resignation and walk away. Somehow they just
don't have it in them to fight dirty or cause a scene.

The way to tell how someone will react is by looking at
the stem of his **d**. There are three sorts:

THE SCORPION TAIL

This is the sign of a venomous tongue. Anyone who draws a **d** with the stem hanging over to the left is a master of the barbed put-down. Sometimes witty, often vicious, these people can silence an entire room with one well-timed phrase – a jibe so withering it leaves you dumbstruck.

If the scorpion tail turns back in on itself like this, at least the individual is trying to keep his temper in check and will manage to bite his tongue on most occasions, despite the overwhelming temptation to do otherwise.

For some, pointed comments are used daily as a means of letting others know who is in charge. In other circumstances, the weapon may only be produced at times of stress. Either way, it is definitely well within the person's capacity to shoot you down in flames if you overstep the mark, and unless you have a similar talent for stinging backchat, then you would be wise to avoid an all-out slanging match – just walk away.

THE ROCKET-LAUNCHER

Whilst the Scorpion-Tail person will usually have the last word in any argument and thus win it by force of personality alone, the Rocket-Launcher simply takes as much as he can of a trying situation. But then, when he is pushed too far and can take no more – BOOOM! – he hits the ceiling. Anger explodes from him in an uncoordinated stream of invective. Tempers fly, as do plates and teapots. Then, quite suddenly – like a rocket after take-off – it's gone and everything becomes peaceful once again. What needed to be said has been said and he is relieved to have got it off his chest. The way is then clear for making up. Before you know it he is showering you with small, silly gifts, apologizing for going off the deep end and promising that it won't happen again.

All this anger is trapped in the loopy stem of a **d**.

The fatter the loop, the more of a display the individual will put on when angry.

The thinner the loop, the greater will be his tendency to suppress anger. The writer will probably go off like a damp firework when roused, with a few odd sparks here and there, before fizzling out altogether in a spectacular display of remorse and cowardice.

THE CONTROL FREAK

A **d** with an upright, unyielding stem means one of two things: i) either the writer is super-calm, a really friendly person with not a molecule of bad feeling anywhere in his body; or else ii) all his strength is being directed into stifling the anger to prevent it reaching the surface. It's difficult to tell which sort is which, frankly, and so you will have to mix this information with signals drawn from elsewhere in the handwriting. However, since everybody has a breaking point, and since no-one outside of a Tweety-Pie cartoon is so mindlessly happy-go-lucky that they can't be pushed over the edge by *some*thing, I would always opt for the second interpretation.

*Other **d**'s to look out for*

(Wriggly stem) Deflects anger, pulls back, rather than launching into attack.

(Tiny bowl with tight loop on stem) Suffers from mean little thoughts and loses temper when protecting his own interests.

(Bowl separated from stem) Stiff upper lip; has probably been brought up to contain anger and so it often goes unexpressed.

(Incomplete bowl) The writer lets it be known that someone has hurt his feelings, but will rarely say anything. May get sulky or start pouting and leave you to guess that something is wrong.

Communication Skills

F

> Capital **F** is an indicator of the force of someone's personality and how proficient he is at communicating his ideas to others.

At heart, a capital **F** is simply an **E** with the sex-bar snapped off the bottom. So it makes sense, when interpreting its meaning, to employ the same criteria we used earlier in relation to the stem and the head- and heart-lines.

Your **F** should be well-proportioned, with the stem strong and upright and the two cross-bars a reasonable length and connected to it firmly. Something like this would do just fine: F.

The **Head-line** represents mental power, the conveying of thoughts and ideas and the lengths an individual will go to to influence people around him.

 An exaggerated head-line, one which stretches out over the next letter in the word, or even beyond, is a positive sign that the writer has faith in what he says and enjoys explaining it to other people. He believes he is right most of the time and is keen that others should accept this to be the case without question. He will probably not welcome a meeting of minds, since he needs to dominate a discussion and have people fall in automatically with his way of thinking. Indeed, he probably *insists* that they listen to him, and gets tetchy if they don't see his point of view and concur with it.

A stunted head-line signifies a lack of conviction and a low turnover of ideas.

A disconnected line means that the writer may at times stick his neck out by suggesting ideas which have not been thought through properly. Even if his presentation is flawless and his enthusiasm enviable, it is always best to check that his proposed plans have sound foundations before acting on them.

When the head-line begins behind the stem and then creeps back over to the other side, it is telling you that the writer brings a wealth of past experience, some good, some not so good, to bear on current problems. He is influenced by what has happened previously in his own life and shapes daily situations to accommodate long-held beliefs. Such an approach can be enormously valuable, always provided these old attitudes do not cloud his judgement and prevent him adapting to new methods, ideas, procedures, etc.

The **Heart-line** reflects the strength of inner feeling brought by the writer to his relationships with others. Deep down, is he sure of what he is saying? Is he passionate about his beliefs or does he agree to anything out of sheer eagerness to please?

The longer and more forceful the heart-line, the more the person relies on gut feeling and reacts from the heart. Consequently his opinions will have a ring of truth about them and tend to make a greater impact on those he deals with.

Once the heart-line becomes overlong and particularly if it pierces the next letter in the word, like this: _fa_, you know that the writer is so passionate about his beliefs that he feels compelled to impose them on others. Taken to its extreme, this is the sign of a loose cannon: someone who may so depend on his own judgement and intuition that he fails to canvass the views of anyone else before going ahead with what he feels to be right.

By contrast, a stunted, insignificant heart-line is a mark of low self-confidence. It tells you that the person does not trust gut feelings and as a result lacks the courage of his own convictions.

Should the heart-line become divorced from the stem, then you need to be guarded about accepting what the writer tells you. He may believe every word of it, but what he is really doing is trotting out the party line – a set of facts he has learned from someone else over the years and adopted as his own. On the one hand, he just might be telling lies; but more likely he has lost touch with what he truly believes and is citing someone else's opinions instead.

Other **F**'s to look out for

(**Large and looming stem**) Forceful and unrelenting in the pursuit of his aims. Everybody is

made aware of what he thinks and believes, and
left in little doubt that to disagree is to invite a
lively discussion as to who is most definitely and
incontrovertibly right – i.e. *him*.

F **(Weak and stumbling backward)** Although the
writer may have plenty to say, for some reason
he just can't bring himself to say it. Probably
lives in fear of criticism and would rather clam
up completely than risk opening his mouth and
embarrassing himself by saying the wrong thing.

f **(Tiny F)** The writer is keen to get noticed but his
voice is simply not being heard. Nor will it ever
be unless he is prepared to sidestep his fears of
being overruled or contradicted and stand up for
what he believes in.

F **(Short head-line, elongated heart-line)** Low on
ideas, probably fails to grasp even the most basic
concepts. Nevertheless he will try to put them
across passionately as though he knows what he
is talking about.

f **(Large loop)** This person thinks too much before
venturing an opinion. He has plenty to say and
will say it forcefully, but his views are a product
of convoluted reasoning and endless self-justifi-
cation.

Curiosity

P

> The capital **P** shows just how nosy you can be,
> or at least how interested you are in other people
> and what's going on in the world around you.

The perfect **P** is a strong vertical stem drawn in a single stroke with a hoop of reasonable size: P, indicating an average level of curiosity. The writer won't pry unnecessarily into other people's affairs, but at the same time will be sufficiently aware of what is happening around him to offer an opinion if asked.

A **P** with a huge, overextended hoop on it, like a giant snout, is a sure sign that this person is almost uncontrollably curious. Anything and everything interests him and no detail will be overlooked, however tiny or insignificant it may seem to others. At its extreme, curiosity turns to all-out nosiness where the writer cannot help himself – he simply *has* to know what's going on and will sniff around relentlessly until he has uncovered every last sordid detail of his friends' or neighbours' lives.

This trait need not be a bad thing. Someone with an unquenchable thirst for knowledge could also be a font of fascinating facts. Always eager to learn new things, he will be riveted by whatever you have to tell him on any subject and positively itching to pass on what he has learned to other people. Whether he later turns those snippets of information into gossip and spreads them around the neighbourhood like confetti is another matter.

If the nose is so big that it dwarfs the stem, and particularly if it extends upward and outward, then the writer is a veritable data-dumpster, collecting information more or less for its own sake. He has a hunger for learning that can never be satisfied. Once he has digested all you have to tell him he moves swiftly on to the next person, and then the next, in his neverending quest for knowledge.

A flattened nose on the **P** indicates a degree of restraint in the writer, or even total indifference to what is happening around him. Events in his own life are probably a priority, and although he may show interest when gossip comes his way he would never stoop so low as to go scratching around for it.

Other **P**'s to look out for

(**Full-sized nose, buckled stem**) Sign of insecurity and weakness. May be curious about other people because he secretly envies them, or because he suspects they may be manoeuvring against him behind his back.

 (**Nose connected to base of stem**) There is a certain amount of restraint involved. The writer may get a secret thrill out of prying into the affairs of others but knows that he shouldn't really. Conflict of priorities prevents him probing too deeply.

 (**Raised nose**) The writer feels unnaturally superior to others and habitually turns his nose up at their lifestyle or concerns. Tends to be quite snooty, even dismissive.

RELATIONSHIPS

Meeting People

u

> To tell whether someone is a 'People Person' and mixes
> well, or has difficulty relating to others, you need
> to look at the way he writes his **u**.

If the **u** is joined to the letters on either side of it, linking
them together…

think he would have been

…then the writer will probably be a good mixer. He feels
relaxed as part of a group, able to chat, make friends and be
sociable. That doesn't mean he won't also enjoy his own
company. We all need time to ourselves occasionally, to
gather our thoughts and pursue more personal interests. Even
so, faced with the right sort of social gathering, the Well-
Connected-**u** person will feel comfortable and blend in well.

  On the other hand, once the **u** becomes divorced from the
letters around it and stands alone, as it does here…

a pleasant country town

...then chances are the writer prefers the more intimate contact of a one-to-one situation, or may even have special interests which can only be pursued alone. As often as possible he will break free of the social round to bask in the private pleasures of a good book, crochet, fishing, the model railway in his attic, or whatever.

A small isolated **u** with a narrow neck is more anti-social. Not only does the writer shun the party circuit, but his private interests are also likely to be extremely narrow. There is little room in his world for new people, distant horizons, fresh experiences or ... well, for life itself even!

Should you ever find a **u** with a lid on it, try not to intrude too much on the writer's time. He will be unnaturally guarded in his dealings with people and shrink away from sharing his ideas and beliefs too freely with them. He lives in a world of his own making to which only a choice few have access. If Mr and Mrs Closed-**u** have bought tickets to a symphony concert, not even Perry Mason could winkle out details of when it is, where it is or who is playing.

Other **u**'s to look out for

(**Small and shallow**) May get on reasonably well with his own crowd, but not an out-and-out People Person. The smallness denotes a lack of vibrancy and a low-key personality.

(**Tight and compact**) This type makes a positive effort to reach out to others, but has limited entertainment value in himself. More likely to drift along with the crowd than be at the centre of it.

Image and Fun:
Spotting the Party Animal

f

> Your little **f** reveals how much you care what people think of your behaviour; whether you can let yourself go and have fun; and how good you are at projecting your personality.

Are you concerned about the impression you make when you walk into a room? Do you feel comfortable meeting new people or does every social encounter throw up a fresh set of horrors? At parties do you hover nervously in the kitchen, sipping a glass of water and listening to some DIY fetishist boasting about his new loft conversion, or are you the life and soul who, once through the door, immediately dives into the crowd and starts networking?

To gain access to this sort of information in someone's handwriting, you need an **f**.

Although it has dozens of variations, I've narrowed them down to two types – i) this: $\mathcal{f}$, which is made up of loops at the top and bottom; and ii) this: $\mathcal{f}$, which is just like a capital **F**, only smaller.

F'S WITH LOOPS

Bottom Loops

The size of the bottom loop on your **f** measures your individuality and tells us whether you are quiet and reserved or have brash, lively qualities that cause you to stand out from a crowd. A big bottom loop usually points to a big personality.

A tail with a bloated loop to it signifies that the writer is a larger-than-life character, someone with a lively image to sustain, who in any social gathering always does his very best not to disappoint. The rule is: the bigger the loop, the more spirited a person will be and also the more carefree about expressing himself.

In making your assessment it is important to note whether the **f** has a forward loop that swings around the front of the stem: , or a reverse loop that curls around from the back: . If the loop is forward, then so is the person – eager to join in, to play the happy party guest and throw himself around to music in the name of having a good time. When the loop is backward, the writer has learned to wait for the right moment to arrive before being too ebullient or frivolous. He will seldom gatecrash an event, and would prefer to be invited formally.

This, with its angles and sheer size, points to someone who privately *yearns* to socialize, to see and be seen. You're dealing with a real party animal here (in this case it's a woman), who will contrive by any means available to be at every social occasion in the calendar. It needn't be a glittering affair – any old event will do. Indeed, on a bad night, she would probably attend the opening of a can of soup, given half a chance.

She may be polite and wait to be invited; then again, such
is her desire to be involved that, if the invitation is not forth-
coming, she will more than likely tag along anyway.

A thin loop signifies individuality too, only with
a less flamboyant edge to it.

The walking-stick **f** means that the writer is not
possessed of a high-octane personality at all
and will hardly set the world alight or take the
trouble to pander to others' expectations. Such a person
boasts a certain individuality which singles him out from
the crowd by setting him apart from it. He prefers to go his
own way and rarely, if ever, does he feel the need to seek
the limelight or to become immersed in current trends. If
some folk are prepared to idle away their lives griping
about the way he dresses or conducts himself, that's their
problem, frankly.

Top Loops:

A top-loop person is more reserved about the way he presents himself and about the effect his behaviour will have
on others. The greater the loop: the greater the degree of
reservation; the smaller the loop: the less time is spent
considering the consequences of his actions.

Individuals who draw large top loops tend to
care what people think of them and are embarrassed quite easily. They don't like to be seen
acting out of character or behaving improperly, and cherish
a desire always to make a good impression. They are pleasant but seldom charismatic and certainly won't light up the
room when they walk in. Rather than grabbing undue attention, they are content to stand by, survey the scene and pick

their moment to become involved.

THE CROSS-BAR

Since cross-bars are only to be found on some **f**'s, I have
left them until last. And in case you're wondering what an
f with a cross-bar looks like, this is it: 𝖿

If the little tail shoots out confidently to the
right, then the writer projects his personality
very effectively. He likes to be appreciated and
so will usually do his best to mix and be good company.

A short, stumpy cross-bar means the writer
may very well be oozing character and personality underneath but, for some reason, has
never quite got the hang of putting it across to others. He
needs to project more.

A reverse cross-bar – one that gets cold feet
and slips out the back way – is a sure sign that
the writer subdues his personality. He may feel
quietly confident about his sense of individuality but for
some reason holds back. He can't or won't share it with
others without some coaxing. Sometimes a few stiff drinks
will do the trick by loosening him up. On other occasions
he may just turn and run.

Above all, please bear in mind that **f**-loops can change
daily. Factors such as stress, worry, fatigue and moods all
play a part. Sometimes you feel outgoing, bursting with
vitality and ready to party, other times you want to stay at
home on your own with the curtains drawn. Your **f**'s will
respond directly to these changing emotions and the shape

of them will vary accordingly.

And finally, a brief mention for the second kind of **f**:

THE SMALL CAPITAL F

Some people write their small **f** like this: $\mathcal{F}$.

However, because it looks like a capital **F**, it conforms to the rules governing capital **F**'s and relates to force of personality rather than image and individuality.

Passion

t

> A single **t** has one purpose only. Using it, we can
> tell whether the writer's emotions come from the heart,
> or whether they are some well-rehearsed act designed to
> impress others and get him what he wants.

Most women are experts in this field.

They don't need teaching the value of being able to express freely their emotions, they know it already. This stuff is second nature to them. Chatting with girlfriends, they regularly open up and lay their feelings bare. What's more, they are constantly attempting to convey those feelings to the men in their life.

Predictably perhaps, many men don't want to know. They shrug off the idea of allowing themselves to be more open, vulnerable and affectionate, dismissing it as 'cissy stuff'. Indeed, such is the frailty of the male ego in modern culture that displays of affection between men are treated even now as an affront to masculinity generally. They get embarrassed by it.

Not all guys think that way, of course. But those who do,

who feel awkward and dodge around this subject whenever possible, are misunderstanding what 'being in touch with your feelings' really means.

People believe us when we act and speak from the heart. Our message carries conviction. And even though others may disagree with the content of what we are saying, they at least respect the honesty with which it is expressed. Therefore deciding whether a writer is tuned into his emotions is a crucial part of the analysis, and one which touches on many other aspects of his character and personality.

A small **t** can be used to measure the level of passion within the writer and to discover how deep those feelings run. Try thinking of the stem as the gauge, a sliding scale, with the mind at the top, the heart in the middle and sex at its base, just as we saw with the capital **E** (pages 76–82) earlier. Then use the cross-bar as a marker.

Ideally, the bar should slash through the middle of the stem, through the heart. The firmer the stroke, the greater will be the writer's capacity for expressing openly what he feels inside. He will speak passionately about matters of deep concern to him, mean every word of what he says and show a refreshing openness in his dealings with others. Furthermore, being romantic, he will be capable of spontaneous gestures of love and affection which are wholly genuine.

At the same time there is a danger of impetuousness. Because he allows his heart to rule his head at times he may not pay sufficient heed to the advice of others, since he believes he knows best, and could come unstuck as a result.

If the slash misses the middle of the **t** and cuts it at a much higher point, the person places less emphasis on feelings and focuses more on con-

cepts and ideas. Affairs of the heart are not a priority here
and take second place to intellectual concerns.

Beware, though: someone with a high **t**-bar will usually
deny instantly that this is the case. After all, none of us
wishes to be thought of as remote or cold or unfeeling. But
the fact remains that, in day-to-day dealings, this person
will be ideas-led, employing logic and reason to guide him
rather than relying on intuition alone.

A slash cutting the stem much lower down indicates that sex is a prime motivator and the writer
channels much of his energy into seeking out
sexual gratification. In such cases, sensitivity will usually
fly out of the window just as rampant lust is marching in
through the door.

Should you discover a cross-bar that is not connected to the stem at all, then the writer has
allowed a certain distance to develop between
what he really feels to be right *in*side and how he acts on the
*out*side. This is usually done by adopting a system of off-
the-peg responses to deal effectively with daily challenges.
They may not represent his natural reactions, but they work
every time and as long as they do, he will keep on using
them. Such people are cruising on automatic, doing what is
expected of them, using their adopted persona to keep the
world at bay.

A theatrical agent who fires up the hopes of his actor
clients by repeatedly telling them that the next job is just
around the corner when in fact he has nothing at all in the
pipeline for any of them, would be a likely practitioner of
the detached cross-bar.

Other t's to look out for

(Floating cross-bar) Not the passionate type; this person inhabits a world of ideas and dreams. Romanticizes extensively, but is not really romantic.

(Curved cross-bar) Has a certain flair and a capacity for showing it, but the writer is held back by emotional links to the past. Needs support and endorsement.

(Disconnected cross-bar overshadows next letter) A stabbing t means the writer uses automatic responses to hurt, attack or control other people. Defensive behaviour rather than heartfelt and genuine.

(Stem swings up to form cross-bar) The writer channels much of his sexual energy into his day-to-day dealings, giving an extra boost to his powers of self-expression. Doubly passionate. May forgo sex and concentrate on communicating feelings verbally.

Affection and Manipulation

K, k

> The **K** has two distinct sides to him: an affectionate side
> that makes you want to run up and hug him, and
> a more manipulative, forceful, deceitful side that
> makes you suspect that he's pulling the wool over your
> eyes. **K** is no fool. In both cases, he knows exactly what
> he wants and plans to get it by hook or by crook.
> You have been warned.

A **K**, big or small, is made up of a stem: $|$, and what looks
like a pair of arms: $\langle$ sticking out of the stem in a sideways
v-shape.

As far as the stem is concerned, it should be firm, straight
and upright. If it isn't, then all the usual rules apply. The
arms, though, are fascinating since they can be interpreted
in two entirely separate ways.

A **K** with arms like this: $\langle$ is a hugging, affectionate **K**.
A **K** with arms like this: $\langle$ is either manipulative or
forceful depending on the size of the arms (see p. 136).

There is plenty of room for confusion here because a person may have both sorts of **K** in his writing. So for the sake of an easy life, let's deal with them separately.

I) THE HUGGING ARMS

Anybody who draws a **K** in this way, where both arms stretch out and are of equal length, is guaranteed to be a touchy-feely person – tactile, warmhearted, someone who lavishes hugs and kisses on all and sundry and who expects to receive as much, if not more, in return.

The wider the arms, the more demonstrative he or she will be; the more outstretched the arms: the further the writer will go to win the hugs and kisses he needs.

Notice how, in each case, the arms begin at the stem and spread outward. *This is important.* The arms should be connected to the stem every time. If they are not, as with this **K** here: then the affection is not genuine, it's just for show.

Among glitzy showbiz types, polite empty kisses, one on each cheek – 'Dahhling! Mwaah! Mwaah! How are you?' – are very much the done thing. However, this ritual is just an affectation, seldom rooted in heartfelt emotion, and only a fool would take it seriously.

People who don't behave so affectedly, yet find themselves in a frothy 'Mwaah! Mwaah!' environment, will often do their bit and kiss friends and others on the cheek too, but only because it is expected of them. Nothing is meant by it. They are going through the motions rather than the emotions, and the arms of their **K** will stand a little distance from the stem to prove it.

If the arms overshoot the stem and begin to the far left of it, you're witnessing signs of a deep emotional craving. The writer can be possessive and selfish, and secretly longs for more affection than he can ever receive. This side of him is kept out of sight, however. There is a certain fear of revealing all which prevents him ever being fully satisfied.

If the **K**'s arms are small or practically non-existent, then your chances of being greeted with a warm, hearty, suffocating hug by the writer are about as likely as receiving a course of ballet lessons from Arnold Schwarzenegger. Fancy displays of kissing and backslapping are not their thing at all, so don't even bother to ask.

II) THE COMPELLING ARMS

Often our problem is to decide whether another person's affection towards us is genuine and heartfelt or just a sham – an elaborate performance designed to mislead or entrap. Well, a good way to tell is by examining the length and curve of the arms on the **K**.

It's easy.

Here we have a straightforward, reliable, honestly affectionate, no-messing-around **K**. It has an upper arm and a lower arm of roughly equal length and both are firm and connected. You feel you could trust a **K** like that, don't you? And you'd be right.

K If the lower arm of the **K** is longer than the top
   one, and especially if it slips underneath the following letter in the word, then, although the person may have engaging ways and come across as sincere,
caring and affectionate, in reality he has
other motives too: perhaps it's just to
get you into bed as often as possible;
or maybe you're dealing with a flash
business executive who will buy you
lunch, win you over with a smile and
some fancy talk, only to clinch a deal
which hammers you into the ground
that very same afternoon.

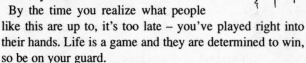

  By the time you realize what people
like this are up to, it's too late – you've played right into
their hands. Life is a game and they are determined to win,
so be on your guard.

  In the end, it's a matter of degree.

K If the lower arm extends out, but not very far, the
   person is only slightly manipulative.

 If the arm goes too far and seems to wrap itself
   around the letter next to it, almost smothering
   the poor creature, you know the writer can be sly
and quite ruthless when he wants to be. Sure, he may have
a likeable, approachable personality on the surface, but
behind that façade he is quietly and carefully working
things out to his own advantage. Whatever it takes, he will
win in the end.

K When the *upper* arm of the **K** extends too far and
   overshadows the next letter in the word, then this
   person is very up-front about what he wants. In

love, he may overwhelm partners with tokens of affection – cards, flowers, perfume, clothes – pouring it on by the bucketful in order to grab their attention and make them adore him more (though this approach can be so stifling at times that it has quite the opposite effect and drives people away!)

This writer will not hesitate to wave the big stick when he feels it is called for. He takes pride in his reputation for firmness and discipline, enjoys ordering people about and cares little for free-thinkers who want to go their own way. 'Toeing the line' is what this guy is all about, which is fine for him maybe, but can be rather heavy going for everyone else.

When the arms are not connected at all, the writer will be short on conscience and possibly quite self-serving in his actions. In extreme cases his behaviour may be devoid of ethical considerations, and this is when your only option is to cut him plenty of slack and keep your wits about you.

Other **K**'s to look out for

(**Looped upper arm**) This is always a sign of someone who cannot bring himself to use coercion when working with others. Persuasion, cajoling, big hints, 'pretty pleases', anything will do, but force is to be avoided at all costs.

(**Firm lower arm, hooked and extended upper arm**) Belongs to a person who is prepared to whip people into line. He makes a stand and is confident enough to ensure that others do as he says. Disciplined and somewhat overbearing, he must have his own way.

Emotional Fulfilment

M, m

There is a world of difference between being merely contented with a relationship and being fulfilled and energized by it. The letter **m** shows the level of satisfaction shared by a married couple or other long-term partners.

Everything I am about to say applies to both big and small **m**'s. However, of the two, we use the small **m** more because it sits closer to the line. The reason why will become obvious shortly.

THE SHAPE OF THE m

An **m** is made up of two hoops squished together.

For a perfect match, the hoops should be pert, alive and blooming: $\mathcal{M}$ like that, indicating that the relationship is on an even keel with neither party dominating, each giving the other space to grow.

The left-hand hoop represents the writer's side of the relationship, the right-hand hoop the partner's side. So if the two hoops are uneven, like this perhaps: $\mathcal{N}$ or this: $\mathcal{M}$, then whichever side of the **m** is *bigger* is the one that 'wears the trousers', so to speak. He or she is the motivator, the engine inside the machine, the one that gets things done.

This sort of imbalance does not automatically suggest problems or dissatisfaction within a marriage.

Let's face it, some men happily succumb to their wife's greater will. They enjoy having their entire life organized by someone else. It saves so much effort. Similarly, some women prefer to be governed and kept by a man and have every last detail of their lives catered for by him. And if this arrangement suits both parties, fine. It's when the imbalance is not part of the deal, when one party resents the other for hijacking the relationship – that is when the trouble starts.

m   Wherever possible, both hoops should be of equal size and pleasantly rounded at the top, indicating a mutual, loving and balanced understanding between two people.

M   If the hoops are *not* rounded, if they're sharp and spiky instead, then it is unlikely that the writer has a deep understanding of what long-term relationships are about. He feels awkward letting himself go the way other folk seem to. In most cases, this type of person has simply not learned to relax. He tries too hard to maintain a strict, organized structure in his world, perhaps because he fears that without such control the marriage would fold in on itself and collapse.

On the plus side: two spiky-**m** people together could hit it off nicely. Since neither will really understand the concept of emotional fulfilment anyway, neither will miss it when it doesn't happen. Their partnership will be built on more rational, down-to-earth foundations.

THE SIZE OF THE m

The size of the hoops on an **m** is important, both in relation to each other and to the rest of the handwriting.

Like plump and risen dough, they should be of equal height with plenty of room underneath: $\mathcal{M}$ – this spells happiness. They should not be leaning dangerously against each other: $\wedge$ or be flattened and demoralized as they are here: $\curvearrowright$, which spells disillusionment.

Also, they should be joined together comfortably midway: $\mathsf{m}.$

Here, although both parties appear to be together, they are each operating as a separate unit within the relationship. Clearly, they lead busy lives in their own individual way, and so use their relationship more as a convenient facility than a lovey-dovey, all-consuming collaboration. This is not a union based on give-and-take dependency.

Where the hoops of the **m** are intertwined and inseparable, these traits will be reflected in the marriage. There is an over-involvement here, and when one party is drowning the other with unwanted

affection or attention it can lead to serious problems. If the
condition is by mutual consent, you will discover two people cocooned in their own little world. They finish each
other's sentences, wear matching patterned sweaters and
bobble-hats in winter, drive identical cars to work and play
tennis doubles in co-ordinated designer outfits that make
them look like dancing book-ends. Sweet, but rather
excessive.

Other **m**'s to look out for

(Ordinary-sized left hoop, tiny right hoop)
Relationship is either over or in a state of tran-
sition. Maybe the flame of love is slowly fizzling
out, or it could be that one of the partners has
died or walked out. Either way, this arrangement
is very one-sided and decisions about the future
need to be made.

(Arched m) Reluctance or inability to form deep
relationships. Being intertwined and involved
indefinitely with another human being holds
minimum appeal.

(Elongated hooked stem) This person has an
idealistic view of relationships which can never
be lived up to. He clings onto a perfect vision
which he has held since his youth, against which
reality is bound to disappoint.

(Backward loop on stem) The writer engages in
far too much thinking and not enough action.
Planning and scheming, fretting and plotting,
always trying to remain in control.

(One hoop only) The writer is supporting his partner. This usually occurs in the case of physical illness where one party has been forced to nurse the other. 'In sickness and in health ...' etc.

Partnerships

th

> A **t** and an **h** together tell us how a person treats
> his or her partner.

In order to make the **th** coupling work, you have to imagine that the writer's feelings and behaviour are embodied in
the **t**, while his partner's reaction is portrayed by the **h**
standing alongside him.

Any word will do: **the**, **those**, **theory**, **Athens**, **zenith**,
fathom.

In each case, if all is going well and the relationship is balanced and flourishing, then the two letters will complement
each other, standing side by side, touching gently: *th*.
They will not be aloof: *t h*, nor will they be intertwined to
the point of suffocation, so that it is difficult to prise them
apart or tell which one is which.

th If the cross-bar slashes right across the **t** until it
overhangs the hoop of the **h**, it means the writer
craves dominance over his partner, and will tend
to be an overbearing presence within the relationship.

th

If the **t** cross-bar reaches out wildly, dragging the **h** towards it, you have the disturbing scenario of one very demanding partner using the full force of his emotions to compel the other to succumb to his wishes. Emotional blackmail may be involved, or it could simply be a battle of wills, one which the writer is currently winning. Whatever lies at the root of it, this is a volatile and potentially destructive relationship packed with imbalance.

th

When a **t** foists itself upon an **h**, and when the **h**, in its turn, seems to be trying *t*o escape and run away, it is telling you that the partner is desperate to break loose.

Unconsciously, we know when our partners are unhappy, yet so often we choose to acknowledge the problem only when it is much too late and the damage is done. 'If only I'd said something sooner ...' we sigh. 'If only I'd realized ...' 'If only I could turn back the clock and make amends ...'

By spotting a fleeing-**h** on the page we can tell instantly that the writer is aware of the situation, even though he may choose to ignore it. To face up to the problem could lead to a shift of balance within the relationship; it might even trigger a break-up with both parties going their separate ways, something he is doubtless keen to avoid.

Tackling the situation maturely and directly, as opposed to letting it slide and hoping in vain for an instant solution, is usually the best way out, and may help avert countless 'if only's', not to mention a few sleepless nights.

Other **th**'s to look out for

th

(**Cross-bar slices high across stem**) The writer is not the emotional type. Being rational in his approach to relationships, he will discuss bonding and passion and romance without ever really understanding them.

 (t and h connected by hoop) The relationship is more likely to be built on mutual respect and the regular exchange of ideas than deep feelings.

 (Sloping cross-bar slashes through h) The writer uses a fierce intellect to impose ideas and plans on his partner. If the partner is turned on by such things, fine. If not, it could lead to ructions.

 (Severely disconnected cross-bar flies over h) The writer is divorced from his true feelings and has problems expressing affection, and is afraid that this may drive his partner away. So he keeps a firm grip, hanging on, maintaining control, always ensuring that his other half never wanders off.

The Secret You

tt

We all have many contrasting sides to our nature.
Quite often we wear one face in public and a
wholly different one when we're with family and close
friends. A **tt** formation highlights the difference
between the two.

A double-t, as found in words such as battle, litter, shatter
and Charlotte, is the most cunning device in the whole
Telltale Alphabet. So much so that, if people were fully
aware of the secrets it reveals, I bet they would have second
thoughts before including it in their writing ever again.

To begin with, let's pretend that Charlotte is waiting for a

bus. Or more to the point, the *letters* in the word Charlotte are waiting for a bus.

Faced with two perfectly ordinary-looking **t**'s, one after the other – *tt* – you'll find that the second **t** (the one on the right) represents the outer person, the face that the writer presents to the world; while the first **t**, standing directly behind it, represents the inner self, the private worries, doubts, fears and regrets.

The trick is to take what you know already about small **t**'s (pp. 130-133) and apply those same rules to the **t**'s in this coupling, only separately this time.

If the first **t** (the left-hand one) is smaller than the second, then the writer may present himself in a strong and impressive way, but behind that façade lurks a rather more reserved, apprehensive figure who is less confident than he appears.

If the first **t** is grander and the more dominant of the two, then appearances are deceptive. At first glance the writer may seem vulnerable and weak, but don't you believe it. He has a steely side to his nature which keeps his feet firmly on the ground, and a strength and defiance of positively Ramboesque proportions.

When both **t**'s are the same size and shape… well, what you see is what you get. If the person seems strong and determined at first glance, then that is very probably what he is. If his **t**'s look like this: *tt*; and he is thoughtful and shy on the surface, don't be surprised if he remains so for as long as you know him.

A firm, strong second **t** with a loopy **t** cowering behind it is a sign that, although the writer may seem confident and decisive on the outside, deep down he is more hesitant and thoughtful and needs time before committing to a specific course of action.

Fidelity and Commitment in Relationships

X, x

An **X**, big or small, demonstrates a person's strength of commitment to his partner and whether he can remain faithful within a long-standing relationship.

A firm, bold, well-defined criss-cross **X** is usually a sign of strong commitment. Or at the very least it means that the person understands the concept of fidelity, trust and responsibility.

A woman, say, with a firm criss-cross **X** is unlikely to be flighty or promiscuous or a perpetual bed-hopper. She might have the urge occasionally, but built into this letter is a genuine heartfelt desire to keep her marital show on the road. Her relationship matters enough for her not to risk jeopardizing it by canoodling with her ski-instructor while her husband's out mastering the Cresta Run, or seducing the gas-man less than a quarter of an hour after her lover has driven off to work. To her, it's not worth it. She's in it for the duration.

𝗑   This is perhaps the least satisfactory sort of **X** to have. So tiny it is no more than a dot on the paper, this is the hallmark of the perpetual drifter, someone who flits from one bed to another in a never-ending string of one-night stands and short-term on-off relationships. There's no pinning this person down. He's here today, and perhaps here tomorrow as well, but the day after that he's gone, leaving a trail of tears in his wake. In fact, he can't even *spell* commitment, let alone fall in with its demands.

𝒳   Another variation: the cutesy back-to-back version. This writer has a naive approach to relationships, one that expects nothing less than total mutual respect and support for all time, with both parties playing their roles equally and democratically. However 'for all time' is negotiable. It may last ten days or a year. After that, as the novelty begins to wear off, it may become this: 𝒳 heralding a difficult situation in which one partner has started to dominate the other; and then finally this:)(where both sides have drifted apart and are now merely co-existing while they wait for the divorce papers to come through.

𝜌   This is also worth looking out for. It has four legs like any other **X**, but two of them are tied together. This tends to herald confusion of some sort – restriction, deception, inhibition – *something* is going on, even if it isn't obvious yet. The person may seem outgoing, fun and slavishly committed, but behind the scenes he is either hung-up about losing his independence or else carrying around a parcel of fears and reservations about what being in a relationship really means. Such people appear to be offering unconditional commitment, but all the time are plotting secret moves to wriggle out of it.

Good in Bed?

V, v

V's, big and small, tell us everything we need to know about how someone performs between the sheets, plus whether or not he or she is an incorrigible flirt and even what sort of sexual track record the writer has.

Now, it is possible that some of you may have skipped the earlier chapters of the book and rushed, panting, straight to this section on sexual prowess – though why you should do that I really don't know. Anyway, if you did, you'll have missed the description of how V's work; so let's quickly recap now by doing the test once again.

If you're in a sitting position as you read this, take a quick look down at your thighs. Are they wide open and inviting, or are you perched primly on the edge of a chair with your knees welded tightly together? Whatever the answer, this same position, believe it or not, translates directly to the way you shape your V.

V Someone with rather narrow, conventional tastes in sex, for whom
a straight one-on-one is quite
enough, thank you very much, will have a
tight, inhibited **V**. Just look at the way
those thighs are clenched together!
Whoever wrote that needs to loosen up and
live a little before it's too late. There are no frills and no
thrills to be had here. The first hint of adventure: handcuffs,
inflatables, Ravel's 'Bolero', and they'll be gone in a flash.

V By contrast, people with plenty of diverse sexual
experiences behind them, who have dated a
number of partners over the years and who enjoy
not only the sex act itself but also the
rituals, the foreplay and everything
else that goes with it, will have a
generous, wide open and inviting **V**.
As the old saying goes, 'Two's company, three's terrific', and the wide-open-
V-person would certainly go with that.

The precise shape of the **V** will vary in direct accordance
with: a) the writer's attitude to sex generally, and b) his
changing moods. Some folk enjoy sex immensely, yet prefer to ration it to days when they feel good about themselves. Sometimes their **V** will be wide open: $\lor$, at other
times protective and closed: $\lor$. That's OK. It just means
that, rather than gorging on a non-stop banquet, they prefer
to enjoy the occasional slap-up meal.

Where the **V** stands alone rather than being connected to
the letters on either side of it: *avenue*, the writer is telling
you that he sees sex as a one-off performance, a bodily
function, there to be used when it suits rather than turned

into a three-day event. Such a viewpoint certainly sounds a little uninspired, wouldn't you agree?

Five specific variations to watch out for are:

The Come-On V. When the right 'thigh' of the **V** curls over at the top and tickles the next letter as it does here, then the writer enjoys flirting and drawing attention to himself. On the other hand, it is most unlikely that you would ever find a curl on an inhibited **V**. Let's face it, someone with a phobia about sex is hardly likely to go out of his way to get it, is he?

The Hard-to-Get V. If the right thigh is longer than the left and slightly overwhelms the letter after it, the writer is either a little guarded about having sex, or may occasionally deprive his or her partner of the pleasure either to heighten the intensity of the eventual experience, or as a sort of emotional bargaining tool.

The Come-and-Get-Me V. Where the right thigh is shorter than the left, you are probably dealing with someone who is rather – how can I put this? – generous with his or her favours. People like this seem hot, ready and full of temptation at the start, but curiously may not always live up to their initial promise.

The Bragging V. This occurs when the capital **V** is large and quite out of proportion to the rest of the handwriting. If the other letters are small and the **V** towers above them, it's a fair bet that the writer boasts a lot about his sexual prowess, but much of this is merely bravado. Don't be surprised if he is not as proficient between the sheets as he claims, or if he turns out to be shy and fumbling and starts sweating profusely before he's even taken his shirt off.

V for Virgin. When the **V** is unnaturally round at the bottom and looks more like a **U**, the writer is either: i) a young virgin, or someone who is still rather naive and inexperienced; ii) a bit too old these days and fast losing interest in the subject; or iii) too drunk to care, too weak to resist and too limp to do anything.

Inhibitions

L

A capital **L** tells us whether or not the writer is in tune with his sexual and emotional sides. Does he see them as perfectly natural or is he ashamed of them and therefore too nervous to express himself openly? How far is he prepared to go in revealing those true feelings to other people?

The basic **L** shape is a right angle, clear and strong, and preferably without a whole load of loops and hooks plastered all over it.

A simple, right-angled **L** means that the writer is open-minded, able to express freely how he feels and not afraid to confront and explore any moral or sexual bogeymen that might rear their heads from time to time.

A right-angled **L** with loops tells you that this writer too is fairly open-minded, whilst also remaining somewhat reserved about certain aspects of his private life. Probably sensible and even over-sensitive, he will be reluctant to blurt out his personal details to everyone within earshot, and will respect other people's right to privacy too.

A hunched-up **L** tends to be a little coy, and belongs to someone who has one or two hang-ups about sex.  These won't necessarily prevent him having it, but there is every likelihood that, due to his upbringing or beliefs, sex now has connotations and associations which prevent him spreading his wings in the way a less inhibited person would.

As is so often the case, it is all a matter of degree, so:

L's in a nutshell

∟ too vulnerable

∟ quite open and forthright about himself

∠ nervous about revealing details

∠ desperate to keep certain things secret

∝ slightly coy about sexual matters

∧ uptight sexually/emotionally but doesn't want the world to know it

∧ help needed!

Possessiveness

J

> The capital **J** shows whether the writer is free and easy
> with people, allowing them to go their own way, or
> jealous and possessive of them.

Try thinking of the average **J** not as a hook-shape, more as
a wide-open mouth. It has a cross-bar and a tail, and the size
of the gap between the two is a measure of the writer's
appetite for friendships. How attached does he become to
friends, loved ones and others?

J   This sort of **J** devours battalions of people but
without ever becoming too committed. He is fascinated by them, but will not be riddled with
uncontrollable jealousy when they flit out of his life. 'Live

and let live' is his motto. And anyway, to his mind, as one old friend disappears, there will always be two or three more on the horizon, ready to take his place.

J If the cross-bar is short, the person is not deeply interested in other people. They flit through his world all the time and may settle for a chat and a cup of coffee, but he makes few demands otherwise. There is certainly never any urge on his part to lock them in his attic and keep them there.

J J In its most extreme form, where the cross-bar is non-existent, you are up against someone who is totally preoccupied with himself and so consumed by his own concerns and worries that other human beings are extras in the unfolding drama that is his life, and so are of merely passing interest.

A closed mouth indicates that this person has little or no room for new people in his life. He has a select band of friends and prefers to keep it that way. He is wary of strangers and, if he should make their acquaintance, it will usually be for a specific purpose and probably quite a superficial bonding, nothing too intimate.

Other J's to look out for

(**Tight lips, like a trap**) Goes in search of people who are necessary and sucks them into his world. Expects loyalty and could get jealous or possessive if they try to escape. This writer needs certain specific individuals around him in order to function.

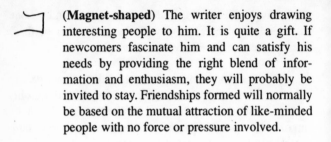

(Magnet-shaped) The writer enjoys drawing interesting people to him. It is quite a gift. If newcomers fascinate him and can satisfy his needs by providing the right blend of information and enthusiasm, they will probably be invited to stay. Friendships formed will normally be based on the mutual attraction of like-minded people with no force or pressure involved.

(Loop instead of cross-bar) Thinks too much, lives in fear of exploitation or betrayal and so is always on guard against false friends.

(Floating cross-bar to the left, like parasol) Constantly searching for people who fit his idealistic values. Rarely finds anyone who can live up to expectations, and so a huge number of acquaintances drift through the writer's life.

(Cross-bar tipped downward) Belongs to a slightly devious individual. He welcomes and embraces many people in rapid succession, but it is usually due to an ulterior motive of some kind. There is something suspicious, sly and underhand about his behaviour, and you would be right to remain cautious until the full picture is made clear.

Responsibility

y

> The **y** is the Gypsy Rose Lee of the Telltale Alphabet.
> It allows you to see into someone else's
> financial affairs and discover what sort of state they
> are in. Is the writer weighed down by debt, or a
> free spirit with few commitments, able to pack his
> bags at a moment's notice and be gone?

THE NO-COMMITMENTS y

A straight vertical stem with no loop at the bottom indicates that the writer feels uncomfortable with too many commitments hanging around his neck, so don't be surprised if he turns out to be single, unattached, with no car, no mortgage and, most important of all, no dependants. This type of person normally pays his bills on time because he hates being in debt to the telephone or gas company. Only by necessity will he ever subscribe to long-term financial plans or loan agreements, and even if he does it will be with the proviso that he could up sticks at

any moment and go to live in another country. Generally he
approaches his affairs with discipline and care, but does not
like to be burdened with responsibility.

Once the stem of the **y** starts to curve around to look like a
tail: $\mathcal{Y}$, then it becomes a reflection of the number of commitments that the writer has taken on – a small mortgage
here, a new car there, he decides to get married or accepts a
promotion. It all adds up.

THE WEIGHED-DOWN-WITH-COMMITMENTS y

$\mathcal{Y}$ By the time the tail has curled right round and
become a full-blown loop, you know for sure
that the writer has amassed as much responsibility as he can possibly handle for now. Because of its
closed nature, he is also unlikely to share the details of it
with the rest of the world. Indeed, if the loop is small and
tight: $\mathcal{Y}$ it points to a whole host of secret responsibilities
preying on the person's peace of mind.
  Responsibility does not have to be unbearable. The writer
may thoroughly enjoy totting up his earnings and outgoings
each month. Some people do – it absorbs them, gives their
life a purpose, a thread. Also remember that
commitments needn't always be financial in
nature. A single parent bringing up a child
alone, a doctor with a large number of
patients, the road manager for a rock
band who has to organize the trans-
porting of many truckloads of equip-
ment between venues each day – these
are all people with commitments who
could well have correspondingly large loops on their **y**'s.

say If the tail of the **y** doesn't form a loop at all, but instead hovers menacingly underneath the rest of the word, then the writer is aware of his responsibilities but is adept at turning a blind eye to the pressure they impose. He may even ignore them, ostrich-like, for as long as he can, whilst remaining aware that they must be tackled sometime. 'Make hay while the sun shines', that's his motto.

It is worth noting, finally, that the cradle of the **y** – the **u**-shape at the top of the tail – offers even more information about how the writer is coping with life's trials.

In its finest hour, the cradle should look like this: *y*, full, rounded and with plenty of space inside. From its openness and size you can tell that the person is enjoying life, living it to the full, and open to new and interesting ways of improving his lot. He has a positive attitude to his affairs and to the way the world treats him.

y A tight, unadventurous cradle is a sign of a slightly underdeveloped taste for what is possible. The horizon seems restricted for this person. He has no appetite for an expansive lifestyle and tends to settle for what he has already, rather than daring to ask for more.

Other *y*'s to look out for

(**No cradle, the y dribbles away across the page**) Life is not providing the kind of all-round fulfilment which the writer deserves. He is busy and quick-thinking but his affairs are getting out of hand. Perhaps he is concentrating on one area of his world to the exclusion of all others. Usually the sign of a workaholic with a packed schedule.

(Tail with sickle on the end) Devious, possibly underhand in dealings. Likes to wheel and deal in order to get through his business life.

(Flicked-back tail) Prevaricates and will put the burden of work on someone else whenever possible.

(Wide-swinging tail) Has trouble keeping affairs in order, but in the end everything gets done and nothing is overlooked.

(Square tail) Practical, no-nonsense approach to financial affairs, never taking on more than he can handle.

(Oversized hovering tail) Secretly worried about the state of finances and other concerns. Problems threaten to erupt at any moment, constantly preying on the writer's mind.

(Inward-sloping tail) Cautious, likes to keep on top of responsibilities. A person who writes this is likely to pay bills ahead of time, keep a constant check on the balance of his bank account, and so on.

The State of the Union: Still Together or Ready for Divorce?

H

An **H** reflects the writer's relationship with his partner. How do the two of them view each other? Are they still functioning as a healthy couple with mutual love and understanding and common interests? Or have the lights gone out these days, leaving them to coast along on automatic?

H'S MADE EASY – THE STEMS

The average **H** is made up of two vertical stems and a cross-bar: H. Applied to a relationship, the left-hand stem represents the writer and the right-hand stem his partner. The cross-bar, by joining the two together, is evidence of the link between them.

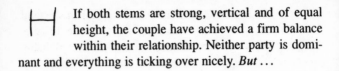

If both stems are strong, vertical and of equal height, the couple have achieved a firm balance within their relationship. Neither party is dominant and everything is ticking over nicely. *But* ...

Once the left-hand stem becomes larger than the right, you know that a lack of balance is developing. The writer is the more dominant of the pair and the partner is standing in his shadow. Actual visible evidence may be slight. Perhaps a number of small things – who earns more money, which one drives the car, who dictates which parties or events they go to – really make the difference, things only the couple themselves would know.

If the right-hand stem is larger, then, as you might expect, it is the partner's interests which predominate. The writer may be in awe of his better half, or just allow him or her to take the lead and make all the major decisions. If the right-hand stem grows *too* large, the other party is making the running. This often happens when the partner is seriously ill and needs constant care and attention. But in all cases, the writer is subject to the whims, needs and decisions of his other half. Fine, if he enjoys taking a back seat, not so fine if he is left feeling small and unimportant.

H'S MADE EASY – THE CROSS-BAR

The stems on an **H** tell only half the story. The true state of a relationship is represented by the way those stems are joined together.

H   A straight **H**, with both stems equal in size and the cross-bar connecting them in the middle, means you are dealing with a mutual relationship based on love, respect and equality.

H   However, if the cross-bar slashes through the right-hand stem without having touched the left stem first, then there is something missing from the romance – a fundamental lack of understanding between the couple. To double-check, try and sneak a look at the handwriting of the partner too, and see how he/she draws a capital **H**. Then compare the two.

H   Similarly, if the cross-bar slashes the left-hand stem but fails to reach as far as the right stem, then although the writer is still committed to the relationship he fears (and probably knows too) that his part-ner is not. Maybe he/she is having an affair, or maybe he/she feels that the spark which was present at the start has now fizzled out. Whatever the cause, a disjointed **H** sug-gests that these two people need to clear the air and sort out niggling differences.

Other **H**'s to look out for

H   (**Clawed left stem**) The writer brings much emo-tional baggage to the relationship and tries to keep a distance between himself and his partner. Regrets, feelings of shame or unworthiness, or just an overall dread of becoming too committed to this one particular person – these are all factors which contribute to such a situation. Communication may have broken down and many vital things be left unsaid for the sake of keeping the peace.

 (**Low-slung cross-bar**) The writer is probably having to support his partner. Illness tends to be the root cause in such cases, and there is certainly an imbalance here; this is not an everyday relationship.

CAREER AND BUSINESS

Achieving Goals

l

> Track down an l in someone's handwriting and you
> can know at once if he has high hopes and plenty of
> plans and ideas, and how likely he is to see them
> through to fruition.

Since a single l is basically a stem and nothing else, you
know that it should, ideally, be strong, perky and upright:
l .

If it is, you are dealing with a writer who has firm plans
for the future as well as a certain number of realistic achievable dreams. Blessed with his fair share of confidence, such
a person tends to have a very definite idea of where he is
going, and, whilst remaining sensitive to changing circumstances and adapting his plans accordingly, he presses on
towards his goals with determination and optimism.

An l which reaches too high and is out of proportion with the rest of the word means that the
person is aspirational, full of bright ideas with

new projects constantly on the drawing-board. His philosophy is: all things are possible. But unless he sets realizable
targets and tackles each idea systematically, none of them
may ever see the light of day.

Stumpy l's are a sign that the writer is not aim-
ing high enough in life. He is a plodder, who
completes the task in front of him before moving
on to the next one, and then the one after that. He has no
long-term game-plan and no idea where he is heading in
life. He is content to stay where he is, do what he's doing,
and leave others to wear themselves out in their frantic pursuit of fulfilment and success.

When the l has a loop to it, the writer is telling
you that he dithers under pressure. So far he has
failed to set the world alight simply because he
hesitates too much before taking action. He is careful and
contemplative and, likely as not, is unable to undertake any
new project without long-drawn-out deliberation. He
thinks, he chews over, weighs up the pros and cons – then,
and only then, does he get down and do it. By this time it
may be too late!

Here the l is tall and looped, and belongs to
someone who is deluding himself about the feasibility of his ideas. He aims high, he shoots far,
but can't see the wood for the trees. Excessive imagination
and a surplus of dreams merely confuse issues and leave
this person without a clear path to follow. If projects do get
completed, chances are it's on a wing and a prayer, and
nobody will be more surprised than the writer himself.

A small l must always be judged in the context of the rest

of the handwriting. Does it tower above the other letters or cower in amongst them? Is it firm and strong or buckled and bowed? If you are still in doubt, then a handy way to back up your judgement is to find a capital **Q**. They are rare, I realize that, but once present on the page they do offer a snapshot of how practical and down-to-earth the writer tends to be.

A **Q** that sits on the line with its tail dangling down to one side belongs to a grounded writer, someone who is slow to indulge in flights of fancy. Plans need to be solidly workable before he will undertake them.

When the **Q** is floating above the line with its tail straight, the writer is telling you that he is a dreamer. He likes to build castles in the air and plan for fantastic eventualities which may never happen. He may be unrealistic about the feasibility of projects and possibly a little unreliable too.

If it helps, think of the **Q** as a helium balloon on a piece of string. A balloon that is sitting on the ground – on the line, in other words – means that the person is practical, reliable and matter-of-fact, whereas a balloon which is floating or drifting away across the writing is an indication that dreams play a major role in the writer's approach to life.

However, if you come across one that is sitting on the line with the string pulled tight beneath it, this simply means that although the writer longs to escape the humdrum responsibilities of daily life, pressures and duties weigh heavily on his mind and he has yet to find a way to shake them off.

Fulfilment at Work

ll

> Double-l is used to measure how happy a person is in his career. Is he fulfilled by what he does or should he be aiming higher? If the writer is frustrated, unhappy, or not making proper use of his talents and abilities, his double-l will give it away.

It is down to each one of us as individuals to root out our true vocation in life – the thing we were put on the planet to do – and do it. Otherwise we may one day regret selling ourselves short. Actors must act, poets must write poetry, plumbers must plumb – it's the way things are.

People who are in the right place, doing the right job at the right time, seldom have problems with double-l's. Assuming you are fired up by what you do, can't wait to get to work every morning, are well-placed for promotion and have a career plan which is working out just fine, then your ll will be strong, bold and look rather like a pair of arms reaching eagerly up to the sky, as they are here:

all the drilling began at 7

shallow A double-l which is too tall, dwarfing everything to either side of it, means that although you may have plenty of aspirations and ambitions, they may be nothing but pipe-dreams. To escape current restrictions, greater discipline is needed. Reassess your goals, trim them down if necessary; be ready to give future plans more thought in order to make them practical and realizable.

follow By contrast, a double-l which is not quite big enough, and which looks as though it has hit a glass ceiling, is a mark of frustration. So if you find something like this in a person's handwriting then clearly his progress is being thwarted by lack of self-confidence, low ambition or even by outside forces – a mean-spirited boss who hates him, or a small working environment with no room for advancement, however good he may be at his job. In all cases, the writer knows that the blockage can't be removed and he must remedy the situation before his dreams fade altogether.

ll Loopy double-l's carry the same interpretation that they do with single l's – too much thought, hesitation and trepidation which lead to the writer being sluggish when seeing plans through to fruition.

Incidentally, it is perfectly possible to have a strong, firm single l: *l* showing that you are positive about your dreams and ambitions, and yet draw a more subdued double-l elsewhere in your handwriting: *ll* , which reveals that your overall prospects are not so good at the moment. In such cases, the answer may well be to continue putting in the proper amount of effort to your current job, whilst secretly nosing around the Situations Vacant columns for something with a better long-term reward.

Taking Charge

to

Do you have what it takes to be the boss?
Can you control a group of people and win their trust?
Together, **t** and **o** demonstrate a person's
managerial skills.

It won't always be possible to uncover a **to** coupling in a
piece of handwriting, but if you do – as in **too**, **token**,
tonight and **torrid** – it tells you whether or not the writer has
qualities necessary to manage a busy office, and how he
deals with and responds to people generally – not just colleagues or employees, but friends, shop assistants, waiters
in restaurants, anybody.

As with previous couplings, the letter on the left, the **t**,
represents the writer, and the one on the right – **o** – the other
person.

When the cross-bar of the **t** slashes through the
stem and joins up to the top of the **o**, the writer
is indicating that he likes to be the boss, and
seeks to control or direct people around him. This kind of

connection is often drawn by someone who seeks to keep others in their place and may not spare their feelings when issuing commands. He means well, but may not be tactful enough. What matters to him is that other people know their position within the hierarchy and, above all, that *he* is at the top of the tree. If he *isn't* top of the tree yet – watch out, because he probably plans to be.

This is very common. The cross-bar of the **t** is detached from the stem and flying wildly over the **o**. At once you can tell that this individual knows all the rules, all the ins and outs of a job, and can be extremely forceful in ensuring that underlings follow them to the letter. Rather than making decisions from the heart he falls back on the rule-book and follows procedures instead.

When the cross-bar of the **t** drops down in an effort to scoop up the **o**, you have a person who enjoys giving a helping hand to those around him, even people who have fallen by the wayside and may never be able to perform effectively. Whenever possible, he will boost morale and help keep the show on the road.

A **t** that seems to be restraining a gaggle of **o**'s on the end of some reins, as in the word 'too**ls**', belongs to someone who is highly adept at supervising more than one person in any environment. He will enjoy overseeing group activities and manage to keep a small company working together as a tight little unit.

Other **to**'s to look out for

(**Disconnected cross-bar, letters widely spaced**) The writer quickly loses control of other people and, in a tight spot, things tend to run away with him.

to **(Unconnected letters)** Not a person who seeks to exert power over others. Likes to be left alone to get on with his own business.

to **(t stooping to touch the following letter)** A person who chivvies others, snapping at them or scolding them when they make a mistake.

to **(t recoiling from the following letter)** If this person gains seniority, he will not feel comfortable exerting his authority. He may not wish to hurt or inconvenience people, or perhaps he is afraid of any comebacks or challenges, in which case many would say that he should not be in charge at all.

Enthusiasm

W

> Capital **W**'s help separate the eager beavers from the idle layabouts, the shepherd from the sheep, the natural-born motivator from the easily-led.

To make firm headway in your career you need a passion for what you are doing, the determination to see it through to a positive conclusion and the enthusiasm to carry you forward even when times get rough and success seems further away than ever.

W reveals how dynamic, committed and excited the writer is about the course he is on.

W A moderate **W** is well-structured, never too tall, never too small, with two arms that reach skyward in a gesture of triumph. This person brings a sufficient degree of enthusiasm to his work to ensure that other people remain confident both in his abilities and in the outcome.

W   A **W** with over-expansive arms tends to belong
      to a person who is enthusiastic without much
      ground for being so. He may be excited right
now about a project, but find it to be unworkable in practice, so he moves on and starts being excited about something else instead. He does not have a firm foundation for
his shifting fancies.

W   A stunted **W** is the sign of moderation taken to
      extremes and probably indifference too. This
      person is far from expressive and will not have
the charisma, the energy or the motivation to drive a task
through single-handedly. He needs to let go of his fears and
allow his natural talents to flow from him, instead of bot-
tling them up.

Woo Wool Once the **W** starts drifting across to the right like
            seaweed until it overshadows the rest of the
            word, you have someone who is not only excited
on his own account, but also keen to motivate and energize
others with his plans. This person likes to be in the driving
seat and will often have the gift of oratory.

Powers of Concentration

r

> The way you draw your **r**'s reveals how good your concentration is: whether you have mastered the knack of focusing your mind on one job at a time, or whether you are easily sidetracked and simply can't do a scrap of work until you know what everyone else around you is up to.

When confronted with an **r** you must first ask the question: does it look up, or is it bent over and staring at the floor?

The perfect **r** looks up. It is perky, alert and unfussy, meaning that the writer is able to keep a firm grip on his work whilst at the same time being aware of what else is going on around him.

By contrast, the floor-starer has its nose planted firmly in what it is doing, bringing 100% concentration to the job in hand. This person is often studious, highly conscientious and never misses a trick. So if you have fiddled your expenses or are planning to slope off for the weekend without completing your share of the work, then you'd better make sure that this guy doesn't catch you at it.

This is known as 'the busybody **r**' – it looks up just a little too much, and belongs to someone who is always chatting, asking questions, interfering, poking his nose into everybody else's affairs. He really can't help himself. Focus and true diligence never were his forte. Sure, he can do the job when it absolutely utterly positively has to be done, but even then, when deadlines are pressing and the boss is baying for blood, the busybody **r** person will still find time to gossip or indulge in office politics.

A shrivelled or crumpled **r** hints at a retiring personality, mild-mannered, disinterested maybe, and far from dazzling intellectually; someone who tackles the work in a methodical fashion and earns his salary at the end of the month, but who will seldom contribute to the thrust and spirit of his workplace.

Other **r**'s to look out for

(**Stem too tall**) The writer has an urge to explore and communicate with others, yet somehow a sense of duty holds him back. He feels that common gossip is beneath him and he exercises restraint.

(**Body of r peeling away from the stem**) By being too inquisitive and concerning himself with matters that are none of his business, this person knows he is going out on a limb. He knows too that he should pull back, but he just

can't help himself. He simply *must* know what is
going on.

**(The r hooks right back over its own shoul-
der)** The writer is afraid of a surprise attack.
Whilst no doubt keeping a wary eye on the job in
hand, he worries lest an opponent or rival comes
at him unexpectedly from behind. Clearly he has
plenty on his conscience and although he will put
on a staunch smile to cover his nerves, he is
deeply concerned nevertheless. Perhaps his past
is about to catch up with him.

Honour and Integrity

t

A single **t** – the letter of passion and heartfelt emotion –
has its part to play in business as well, by revealing
whether a person is genuine and to be trusted or likely to
cheat and manoeuvre to reach his own secret ends.

Central to this, as always, is the cross-bar, and whether or
not it connects to the stem.

You know where you stand with someone who
crosses his **t** right through the heart. It is a badge
of sincerity. Of course, whether you then go on
and trust his sincerity is up to you. But at least when he
speaks, he does so with integrity and conviction.

However, if the bar is disconnected and flying
off into mid-air like a spark, then you are advised
to be on your guard. This person is unlikely to be
in touch with his emotions and so may sidestep professional
ethics by saying and doing whatever he believes is necessary to close a deal.

In extreme cases, the detached cross-bar is the hallmark of a swindler – someone who borrows money and promises to pay it back within a week, but never does; an estate agent who sells you a beautiful house without revealing that it will have to be knocked down in three months' time to make room for a new six-lane motorway. Some people simply don't listen to their conscience. They like to think of themselves as tough and shrewd, and equate all that soppy sentimental 'heart' stuff with weakness – with not being able to think straight or 'go for the jugular' when tough actions are called for. Emotions, to their mind, simply get in the way.

Someone with a high cross-bar can be relied upon for bright ideas and stimulating conversation. He will talk around a subject and flesh out the basic structure with concrete proposals.

If the cross-bar is floating idly above the stem, it indicates that the person you are dealing with may have delusions of superiority and feel he can outwit others with his wildly imaginative ideas. The disconnection tells you he may not be reliable. His ideas could prove wholly impractical and his belief in them fleeting. By all means act on the things he tells you – but double-check them first!

Vision and Foresight

i

Your **i**'s relate to your vision. Specifically, how you dot an **i** tells us whether you have a good clear overview of work situations, or whether, in fact, you can't see the wood for the trees.

There is no such thing as a perfect **i**.

It should have a short, straight stem with a dot above it somewhere: *ί* , but it is the exact placing of that dot which determines what kind of approach a person brings to his work.

Generally speaking, a dot sitting above the stem indicates a mind that is focused on the here and now. A dot to the left of the stem displays an undue preoccupation with the past, while a dot to the right means a healthy concern for the future and the way things are going.

For reference, here are the main types.

ί   (**A high dot directly above the stem**) A good, all-round perspective on what is happening. Keeps an eye on several jobs at once. May be lacking in awareness of future possibilities.

ı´   **(High dot to the right of the stem)** Interest in the way events are moving. Concern for the future; likes to plan ahead and get involved in decision-making process.

`ı   **(Dot to the left of the stem)** Too concerned with the past. Yesterday figures strongly in his thoughts, tomorrow hardly at all.

ı   **(No dot)** Scatterbrain. Mind all over the place. Thinks of today, yesterday and tomorrow in rotation. Plans a bit, muses a bit, reminisces a bit. Needs focus and discipline.

i   **(Big stem with dot sitting right on top)** So blinded by immediate pressures and tasks, he can't even see as far ahead as teatime.

i   **(Insignificant stem with dot sitting on top)** Not an expansive thinker. Small details fascinate, but he is not switched onto, or energized by, the bigger picture.

ı`   **(Uses a small streak instead of a dot)** Doubtless intended as a stylish decoration, but it means that, though the writer takes an interest in future plans, he is also rather nervous of what adverse changes and excess pressure they might bring. Tends to be rather self-protective.

ı°   **(Circle instead of a dot)** A naive, innocent, basically uncomplicated person who may be an adult on the outside but is still fairly underdeveloped inside.

Ambition

R

A capital **R** reveals whether you have the right blend of
determination, courage and enthusiasm to make you a
success at work, or are being held back by fear and
insecurity.

Have you noticed the way some people don't just *live* life,
they positively attack it? Charging at the world with all
guns blazing, sailing gracefully over each and every obstacle, fearlessly taking failure and pitfalls in their stride.

With their confidence unshakeable, their pace unstop-
pable, they march on towards their goals, paying little or no
attention to what any Doubting Thomases may have to say.
In fact, the no-can-do attitude which causes so many of us
to fall by the wayside seems only to fuel their stamina and
drive them through to greater success.

Now, it may be that you recognize yourself here. Perhaps
you are a super-achiever. If so, great.

But while you're lounging back, luxuriating in the warm
glow of prosperity generated by your success, you might
spare a wee thought for all those poor no-hopers still lan-

guishing, exhausted, at the end of the queue: the ones who charged at life with all guns blazing, only to run out of ammunition halfway; who saw the pitfalls coming a mile off, and yet still fell headlong into them; who, when they ran across those Doubting Thomases en route, not only listened to what they had to say, but actually took them home and married them.

To find out if someone is ambitious and determined to succeed, you need a capital **R** and its three components: the chest: ⊃ , the leg: ＼ , and the stem: ／ .

THE CHEST

The larger and more puffed-out the chest on the **R** is, the more fearless the writer will be.

R So a chest this size, especially if it overshadows the rest of the word, means that the person has a firm idea of what he wants and pursues it boldly, perhaps even selfishly, to the exclusion of everything else. He is spirited, pushy and direct. Other people's concerns and feelings are secondary to his own achievement. All that matters is forging ahead and grabbing what he believes to be rightfully his.

R The opposite occurs where the chest is deflated and weak. This points to a little too much humility on the writer's part. He allows others to do the running for him and is afraid to appear overambitious, or to stick his neck out and say his piece. Also, he would rather not start ordering other folk around, in case they resent it or he gets put down or ridiculed. He cares passionately what friends and colleagues think of him, and certainly wouldn't wish to antagonize them by insisting that they do something that they don't want to.

R If the chest is puffed out but also pulled back behind the stem, then fears or negative experiences sown in the distant past are still hampering progress, and explain why he can be so forceful and overbearing at times. It is an act of overcompensation for his weakness, yet, curiously, such lingering negative emotions may be sufficient to spur him on to even greater success.

R Where the chest is weak and pulled back behind the stem, difficult lessons learned in the past prevent the writer making progress. They disempower him, hampering his efforts at every turn, filling his mind with the possibility of defeat where none actually exists. He needs to be more positive about his role in life and focus on future success rather than past failure.

THE LEG

Now, you may be armed with all the fascinating chest-facts in the world, but you still can't offer an all-round verdict on the strength of a writer's ambition until you have added details deduced from the leg of his **R**. The longer the leg: $\mathcal{R}$, the more the writer will want to tackle projects or plans step by step, moving forward confidently but prudently and systematically.

R A leg this size shows that the writer makes progress a day at a time. His strategy may be a little hit-or-miss on occasion, but he likes to think he knows where he's heading. For him, the journey cannot be rushed, especially when certain matters or issues are themselves unfolding slowly. Imagine a blind person with his stick stretched out in front of him, unsure of the terrain ahead but making the best progress he can towards his destination. That sums up the writer with an extended leg on his **R**.

R It follows, then, that a stumpy leg will be drawn by someone who is cautious and seldom goes out on a limb. He doesn't really know where he's going and may not even understand the framework within which he is working, but he plods on anyway, taking one tiny step at a time, never overcommitting himself, always hoping that things will turn out for the best. He may be unable to handle too much pressure.

Rather If ever the leg reaches out and slides right under the rest of the word, a red warning light should come on in your head immediately. It is telling you that the writer may be manipulative and devious and although he may appear to be using conventional steps to achieve his aims, he probably has another agenda and may well be employing all manner of underhand tactics to ensure he wins and others fail. And 'others' could include *you*. Forewarned is forearmed!

The same rules about stems apply as always. In deciphering the messages contained in the **R**, take the chest, the leg and the stem separately, decide what each one is telling you and then combine the results into your overall portrait of the writer.

LIFE GENERALLY

Optimism

p

> A small **p** expresses expectation, a sense of wonder and a positive, open attitude to whatever the future may bring.

At its best, the **p** should be bold and uncomplicated, like this: ρ, in which case the writer will be less cynical than most.

A bold-**p** person carries with him a belief that, no matter how difficult things may be at present, everything always turns out OK in the end. And, strangely, by ignoring the doom merchants with their daily predictions of disaster and choosing to remain optimistic, his faith is usually rewarded. Expect the worst and that's what you're likely to get, but expect the best and the best may well fall right into your lap.

On top of this, a true optimist will also have handwriting that slopes gently upward across the page:

Elaine Styles is very nice

When the stem of the **p** is looped rather than a single stroke of the pen, the writer, despite maybe wanting to believe that the best will happen, is nevertheless riddled with reservations and worries. 'Things went wrong last time, so they're bound to go wrong again,' is the way he looks at things. They may well go wrong and live up to his expectations.

If the **p** is written in such a way as to appear to be resting its chin on the letter in front of it, then the person will need plenty of encouragement to help keep his spirits up.

The opposite is true when the **p** links to the following letter from above. Here the writer's hopes and dreams are, to a certain extent, self-propelled. Setbacks are taken in his stride. Nothing is allowed to stand in the way of the ultimate goal. He accepts both success and failure as they come, extracting from them any lessons he feels need to be learned, and then applies them in the furtherance of his overall aims. Nothing keeps him down for long.

Other **p**'s to look out for

(**Shepherd's crook**) Easily led, could be persuaded to follow a course of action which others are convinced is correct, but which may not be. There's a kind of innocence, of constantly hoping for the best, which makes the person concerned vulnerable to exploitation.

(**Hugely overblown head**) Very optimistic to the point of being blinkered. Will not be able to see the wood for the trees. Indecision strikes just as clarity of thought is called for. Too many options present themselves, all of which seem to offer great prospects. Deciding which one is for the best could prove difficult.

(Tiny) Either has a deeply pessimistic outlook on life, or else he has forgotten how to dream. Many times he won't even *try* to see the good in people and situations, preferring instead to assume the worst and expect to fail hopelessly, or be ripped off, criticized or cheated out of his due. Generally, a small mind with narrow expectations.

(Cowering) Belongs to someone who resists making premature judgements. 'There may be good times ahead,' he'll say, 'but let's wait until they get here before we go making definite plans.' He would never admit to being cynical or pessimistic, of course. Instead, he'll call himself a realist and urge you to follow suit if you don't want to get your fingers burned.

(Overlong stem) The writer is affected by a catalogue of hidden considerations. He has been taught to expect the best but finds that life doesn't always fulfil one's expectations. Over the years he has acquired a range of fixed standards and perceptions which he now uses as a blueprint and against which all fresh experience is set. Anything that doesn't measure up is rejected or scorned.

Contentment

b and B

A small **b** and the bottom half of a capital **B** relate to possessions and territory. They show whether you are contented with what you have or, if not, how grasping and selfish you can be.

Think about it for a moment.

Are you really contented with your lot right now? Your home, your belongings and your earnings? Or are you constantly reaching out and grabbing for more? And if you haven't got enough of what you want is it because your expectations aren't high enough and, like Eddie Average at the start of the book, you are forever settling for less than you truly deserve?

If you want something, do you go right out there and get it, or are you too proud to ask? Are you free and easy with your belongings? How do you react to other people stepping in and taking stuff from you? Do you stand and fight or just turn the other cheek?

This particular arena is occupied by **b** and **B**, each supplying different snippets of information.

POSSESSIONS AND TERRITORY
b

The perfect small **b** should consist of a strong vertical stem: with a full, but not overfull, bowl: ⊃ nestling against it.

This is a prince amongst **b**'s. Simple, with no breaks or unnecessary loops or kinks in it, it tells the reader three things: 'I am happy with what I have, I deserve what I have, and I intend to hang onto what I have.'

If the **b** is decorated with a slash that cuts across the bowl and onto the next letter, it means that the writer recognizes a good opportunity when he sees one and will not be slow to stake his claim to whatever he desires.

Now for the bad news.

Most **b**'s don't look anything like that. They're either too small or too bloated, too convoluted or too emaciated.

A shrunken, overmodest **b** is evidence of feelings of unworthiness. The writer doesn't believe he deserves more than the basics. He constantly shies away from requesting a better deal for himself and therefore would be well-advised to reassess his values and priorities to see whether it isn't time to start demanding more from life. A course in assertiveness training would do him no harm either.

A **b** with a swollen bowl and a weedy little stem belongs to someone who treasures the good things in life and does not intend that they should ever be taken away. The writer is outwardly possessive as a way of compensating for deep insecurity: he sees 'things' as a ready substitute for emotional fulfilment, and will always keep an eye out for offers and bargains. Once they are his, he protects them fiercely.

One of the most common **b**'s is the upturned shepherd's crook, where the bowl loops around but never joins the stem. This means that the writer is open to anything new that comes his way. He seeks to improve his lot and does so eagerly, maybe even to the point of being grasping.

This is particularly true whenever you find a crook-shaped **b** grabbing hold of the letter that follows it:

See how the **i** is being dragged back by the **b**? A sure sign that the writer wants more for himself, even to the point of being aggressively acquisitive, and also defends his territory and belongings almost fanatically. 'None shall pass' is his motto, and you would be wise to take note.

So that deals with the writer's desire for possessions and territory. However, when it comes to the *manner* in which he goes about acquiring them, that is embodied in the bottom half of the capital **B**.

GETTING WHAT YOU WANT
B (Bottom Half only)

The bottom half of a capital **B** is a good gauge of how forceful the writer can be in pursuit of his goals or desires. (The top half, which displays a person's pride, is dealt with separately on p.199.)

Ball Something round and bulbous like this, which overwhelms the other letters in the word and looks quite out of place, is a sign that, when push comes to shove, this person can push and shove with the best of them. The fact that other people might find his aggressive, uncompromising tactics irritating doesn't seem to bother him in the least, or if it does he never shows it.

And it certainly won't stop him from pursuing similar tactics in future. When his heart is set on a particular course he behaves like a fairground dodgem car, barging through, knocking all obstacles out of his way in an effort to fulfil his needs.

Such people can be difficult to live and work with since they constantly seek to have their own way. Their desires must predominate. Anything less makes them frustrated and angry. And if – oh boy! – *if* by sheer bad luck there is only one can of Coke in the drinks machine and both of you want it, well, I'm afraid you are either going to have to fight to the death for it, or else back down and let the Bulbous-**B** person have the can without argument. Remember, your needs are secondary. 'Either put up or shut up' is the message here.

Bo If the **B** joins onto the next letter with a slash, then this person will not hesitate to ask directly for what he wants. And if he doesn't get it? Well, I leave that to your imagination – just make sure the Red Cross is on hand to pick up the pieces afterwards, that's all.

B A subdued, inadequate lower bowl on the **B** means the opposite – someone who is too diplomatic, not pushy enough. As a result of being overly wary or apathetic, he may miss out on the better things in life. By trying that little bit harder, by not being so aloof or frightened of rejection, he might find that the direct approach pays off. Asking for something is the only way of letting others know that you want it. If they don't know, and if they don't happen to be clairvoyant, how can they give it to you?

Pride

B (Top half only)

> The issue of pride is an important one. Is the writer too proud, for instance, to ask a favour of someone, or to request the repayment of money when it is owing? Once he has made a decision, will he stick to his guns or simply cave in at the first sign of a challenge?

The answer to these questions lies in the top bowl of a capital **B**.

There is no right or wrong size for it. Whichever way it is drawn, it will indicate how proud a person tends to be: proud of his home, his family, his standards, his country, his principles, his dress sense, his expertise at work ... all bundled up neatly and packaged into one sweep of the pen.

Something resembling a puffed-out chest, prominent and busty like this, indicates huge amounts of pride. Its effects will trickle down into his mannerisms, attitude and the way he conducts his affairs. Once he has made a decision, it would take an Act of God before he would consider going back on it. He will

do things on principle because they are right, and will stick
to what he believes in.

B   Someone who produces a more flattened, more
composed chest is fairly compliant in his behaviour. He adapts his decisions to suit others, likes
to fit in, and will rarely take a stand on a matter of principle.
Furthermore, if he is shown to be wrong, he will be prepared to reconsider his argument or viewpoint.

Other **B**'s to look out for

B B   **(Body of B hooks back behind the stem)**
Influences from the past fuel this person's pride.
He lives his daily life with one eye glancing back
over his shoulder at his upbringing and allows
old standards to affect his judgement.

b   **(Unnaturally high stem)** The writer fails to live
up to the promise of his abilities. He shrinks
away from demanding the best and settles for far
less.

Generosity and Kindness

O, o

A letter **O**, big or small, is the letter of caring and sharing. It shows how sensitive, open and generous the writer can be.

An **O** should be clearly written first and foremost, and be full and plump and round: O . Indeed, the rounder and clearer the **O** is, the nicer the person will be, as a rule.

Even if the rest of the handwriting is all over the place, and looks like palm trees in a hurricane – *flowing* – no matter. If the **O**'s are cute and perfectly rounded, you're dealing with someone who has a core of decency, sensitivity and even innocence about him. He may not always show it, but it's in there nonetheless.

In most cases he will be quite generous too. And by generous, I don't just mean how often he makes donations to charity. That can be done for tax reasons or with a cynical edge. Generosity in this sense spreads far wider and includes giving of himself, his time, his attention and his patience. It means having concern for others, encouraging people when they're down, lending a receptive and understanding ear to someone in trouble.

○   The smaller the **O**, the more closed and self-
serving the writer is and the more he will be con-
cealing his generous nature. Logically, Ebenezer
Scrooge would have an **O** this size: ○ , whilst Bob
Cratchit's would be more like this: ⟨⟩, I guess. That's the
difference.

○   If the **O** has a lid on it, the writer experiences
problems with the very notion of giving and letting go of what he has. Underneath, he may want
to give, but something stops him – probably the instinct to
hang on to what he has at all costs.

○ ○   Constricted or misshapen **O**'s, or **O**'s with dark
○ ○   shadows, pockets or other frills inside them
highlight undercurrents and fears in the writer's
mind. Perhaps his generosity is fuelled by ulterior motives,
perhaps he prefers to save for a rainy day. Perhaps he's just
obsessed with value for money rather than with the good his
generosity would do. Either way, these are not healthy positive signs.

Without doubt, a plump, round **O** is best every time.

Praise

j

> The occasional pat on the back does wonders for your self-esteem, and the quickest way to tell if someone needs and enjoys praise is by looking at his small **j**'s.

Whoever we are, whatever we do, we all need a little recognition of our worth from time to time. Nothing too heavy, a quick compliment will suffice – 'Hey, you completed that job on time. Well done,' or 'You're a brilliant party host', or 'I love your clothes – you've got such a great sense of style.'

Some people crave this kind of confirmation – as Mark Twain once said, 'I can live for two months on a good compliment' – while others find it embarrassing and try to avoid it. Luckily, the letter **j** is here to help you tell which is which. There are five sorts.

The Satellite Dish j is curved but otherwise uncomplicated, with a small loop wriggling away at the bottom. This person likes to be praised and certainly won't let cynicism stand in the way.

Indeed, so keen is he to receive appreciation that he may well go out of his way to earn it, by doing good turns for others, cooking meals, buying presents – no job is so small that it can't be done well and earn a hefty and honest dollop of praise.

The **'Stuff and Nonsense!' j** has a straightish body and a large loop swinging underneath. This is the trademark of someone who doesn't really crave praise at all. He feels he has no need of it and may well dismiss your efforts as a pointless waste of time. The writer believes that, since he operates out of all the right motives anyway and always does his best, a compliment on top of that amounts to too much icing on a very small cake.

The **'Oh, it was nothing' j** has a tail which hugs the stem. The writer is too self-deprecating and denies himself the full pleasure of a genuine compliment. He sees his meagre efforts as inconsequential, or at least pretends that to be the case. Any form of appreciation, though secretly welcomed, is met with a flurry of excuses and deflections.

The **No-Praise j** includes anything small and fiddly. This person will shrug off a compliment, saying either, 'Not interested, don't need it,' or, 'Never had it, won't miss it.' It is highly introverted and evidence of low self-esteem as well as a somewhat limited expectation of success and fulfilment.

The **'Who – me?' j** has a rounded tail with a strange finger-like curl on the end of it, pointing inward. Here the writer is telling us that he feels utterly undeserving of any praise at all and can't believe it when a compliment is shot his way. The moment he receives a pat on the back, he is plunged into a downward spiral of denial: a reaction typical of somebody who was deprived of praise as a child.

No matter how hard he tried to please back then, his efforts were met with anything from indifference to unqualified disapproval, either from parents or teachers or from other adults he respected. So years later, as an adult, when confronted by a genuine heartfelt endorsement of his talents, he finds he has no reference point for dealing with it.

Criticism and Judgement

z

A small **z** measures a person's willingness to criticize others and whether he can make on-the-spot decisions.

Many people enjoy taking others to task. They derive enormous pleasure from pinpointing faults or weaknesses, and will spare nobody's feelings when expressing their disdain over a bad choice of clothes or a piece of shoddy workmanship. Without doubt scathing criticism is great fun for the person dishing it out, but when the tables are turned and the critic himself comes under fire, you'll find he seldom has the constitution for it.

It helps, therefore, to know whether or not the person you are dealing with is someone whose judgement can be trusted, and the small **z** shows this better than most.

There are two kinds: the standard one: Z, resembling the mark of Zorro, and the long dangly one shaped like a figure 3: 3 which usually hangs down below the line like a gorilla from a branch, interfering with the words underneath.

The Mark of Zorro belongs to someone who is bristling with opinions which he simply must share with the rest of us. His great talent is for making snap judgements on the spur of the moment – spouting ready remarks and decisions which go right to the heart of the situation, helping to relieve a crisis, solve a problem, or clear the air when discussions have become tense or reached an impasse.

These gems of observation may not be thought through with great care but they are worth listening to nevertheless, and will no doubt prove to be right when the dust has settled.

If the **z** reaches out too far towards the left, the writer is not content merely to offer his opinion, he absolutely *must* give it, and goes out of his way to influence those around him. Such interference is seldom well-received, I need hardly add.

If the **z** recoils to the right, the writer hesitates before criticizing and positively dreads the consequences of speaking out of turn.

The Swinging Gorilla belongs to a person who uses his knowledge or judgement very carefully. If the top loop of this **z** is bigger than the bottom loop: ３, the writer does not possess huge reserves of knowledge or experience and so needs to think through every decision with great care. If, on the other hand, the bottom loop is bigger than the top one: ３, he is probably a sage, a font of acquired wisdom, able to spout instant advice on what needs to be done without resorting to lengthy deliberation. Somehow he just knows.

3 A z of this kind should not be leaning backward. If it is, there will be a certain reluctance on the writer's part to dispense his advice.

3 If it leans forward, he is more than eager to let you know what he is thinking.

3 If both loops are small and roughly the same size, you have a cocktail mixed from the two: three parts deliberation to four parts wisdom – unshaken and rarely stirred.

33 A big, lumbering z means that the individual has elevated his talents to a messianic level by becoming a fearless purveyor of sensible advice. He can be quite vocal and possibly aggressive in defence of his beliefs, even if they later turn out to have been wholly misguided. Take what he says with a pinch of salt.

Sensitivity to Criticism

q

Beside being a measure of the writer's sensitivity, a small **q** will show you how adept he is at selling himself and putting his ideas across. Does he have the courage of his convictions? Will he take personal attacks to heart, or keep trying until he wins through and gets his own way?

For the best results, your **q** ought to stand upright. It should have a bright, full face, a strong stem and a little tail sticking out behind it at a healthy angle: *q*.

Something like that.

When someone draws a basic **q**, he is reasonably confident in his opinions and ideas and is keen to express a viewpoint. He copes well with rejection, viewing it not as an attack on his value as a human being, more as a stepping-stone to finding the right solution.

q **The queasy q** – so called because it shrinks away from any form of confrontation. See how it recoils, terrified, with its wiggly tail tucked in behind the stem and its head jammed back as far as it will go. It may have an excellent proposal to put forward, but when the time comes to speak up and sell the idea, it is just too scared to try.

A queasy-**q** person secretly fears rejection of any kind, almost to the point of phobia. This is because he tends to see the word 'no' as an all-out assault on his integrity. The merest whisper of the word shatters what's left of his confidence, plunging him into paroxysms of self-doubt.

Take it from me, people who write their **q**'s in this way do not make very good insurance salesmen.

SAMPLE SALES PITCH

KNOCK ON DOOR. DOOR OPENS.

Salesman: Good morning, sir, would you like to buy an insur...

Customer: No.

Salesman: No, of course you wouldn't. Sorry about that.

Customer: Anything else?

Salesman: N-n-no, I think that about wraps it up. S-s-sorry to trouble y...

DOOR SLAMS

Salesman: ...ou.

That is one end of the spectrum. At the other, chomping at the bit, stands...

The rampant q. There's no messing about with this person. With his stem firm and straight, his tail poised and his head straining forward, he is thrilled and exhilarated by the very prospect of putting his message across. He has got something to say and, moreover, is convinced that people want to hear it. And even if

they *don't* want to hear it, he'll tell it to them anyway. Why?
Because Mr Rampant-**q** believes in his product. In fact, Mr
Rampant-**q** *is* the product. First and foremost he is selling
himself.

SAMPLE SALES PITCH

KNOCK ON DOOR. DOOR OPENS.

Salesman: Morning, sir. And what a wonderful morning it
                is. Alas, tomorrow morning may not be so won-
                derful. Therefore might I suggest one of our
                'Wonderful Mornings Guaranteed' policies?
Customer: No thank you.
Salesman: See? Already you're warming to the idea. May
                I step inside for a moment?
Customer: No, clear off.
Salesman: Coffee? I'd love one. Thanks.
Customer: Look, I don't want an insurance policy!
Salesman: Uh-ho! They all say that. Now, if you'd like to
                sign here, here, here and ... oh yes, here.
Customer: Leave now, or I'll break every bone in your
                body.
Salesman: No problem, sir. I'm insured. I'm also a judo
                black belt, incidentally.
Customer: Oh ... er, right. So where do I sign?

Somewhere between the recalcitrant, quivering wreck and
the gushing, superabundantly confident dynamo, lie the rest
of us, with our average, so-so **q**'s.

q   If the face of the **q** is flattened, the writer may
       have the right spirit in presenting his ideas, but
       be unable to put them across with sufficient con-
fidence. Previous rejections still cloud his views.

q When the tail is tucked up behind the stem, you are dealing with a person who either likes to play his cards close to his chest, or else considers his ideas to be so shaky that, to his mind, they don't deserve to see the light of day anyway.

Deciphering the meaning of a **q** becomes altogether tougher when the writer has a distinct forward or backward slant to his handwriting. Opinions vary, but in my experience the best approach is this: ignore the letters on either side, concentrate solely on the **q**. Ask yourself: does it slope forward or backward? What's its tail like? Is the stem straight or kinked?

Never lose sight of the fact that, when the chips are down, someone who is fairly introverted may still be able to summon up sufficient courage to sell himself and his ideas to others. Conversely a person with great ambition and drive, someone with extremely forward-slanting writing, may trip and fall at the final hurdle through a simple lack of faith in his own ability.

Defensiveness

w

A small **w** shows how defensive the writer can be when attacked or asked to justify his opinions or behaviour.

Defensive people can be difficult to deal with. They cling on doggedly to their point of view, not necessarily because they care whether it's correct, but simply because, having expressed it, they feel they must stand by it for all time.

When questioned or criticized, however mildly, they react as though mortally wounded, launching into a tirade of self-justifying counter-attacks until you back down and withdraw the remarks they find so objectionable.

Defensiveness shows up in the right arm of the **w**. The larger, rounder and more bulbous it becomes, the more touchy the writer will be and the greater his desire to justify his words or actions.

So this *ω* is extremely defensive

this *ω* is fairly defensive

this *ω* blends defensiveness with a fear of going too far and risking any comebacks this ω is average; not easily provoked

and this W may be a bit of wimp; certainly not one for engaging in a battle of wills. Listens to other people's opinions, takes on board what they say and adapts accordingly. Likely to be polite, considerate and deferential...

whereas this h belongs to someone who feels that other people don't live up to his own high aspirations and so he nags and cajoles, bickers and even begs them until they fall in with his opinions and demands.

Deep down, a defensive individual feels insecure about some aspect of himself – his looks, his abilities, his overall success or failure in life – so when a casual comment hits a highly vulnerable point, then... BINGO! He will see red immediately, and go to unreasonable lengths to justify his position, even though he may know the other person to be right.

More serious still is when the defensive person starts *over*compensating for his weakness by bullying others. When this happens the right arm of the **w** reaches across and drags in the letter that follows it. Example: $\omega\Gamma$.

See the force being exerted by the **w**? Enough to pull the **i** right off its feet. From this you can tell that the writer is not only highly insecure, but has decided to protect himself by ordering other people about, directing them, urging and cajoling them. He takes on the role of motivator without being invited and .will tend to get his own way on the strength of his personality alone.

Resilience

a

How good are you in a crisis? Or, more to the point, how resilient are you in the face of life's unexpected twists and turns? Do you bounce back with a vengeance or fold up at the first sign of adversity, leaving someone else to clean up the mess? That's what **a**'s are all about.

a   Here we have a good **a**, one with a firm, straight backbone and a fully rounded bowl pressed right up against it. This person is resilient. He weathers the storms of life well, repairing any damage as he goes. He learns whatever lessons are there to be learned, then sails on courageously towards the next experience, undaunted.

a   Where the stem and the bowl are peeling away from each other it means that any show of courage is for display purposes only. In fact he is easily hurt, takes rejection or setbacks personally and has learned to cope only by putting on a brave face, hoping that nobody peeks behind the façade and discovers how insecure he really is.

a An overblown **a** is also a sign of pretend-fearlessness. This person has learned to face life head-on and bowls through obstacles or setbacks as he encounters them. Although most of his attitude is pure bluster rather than strength of character, if it takes him where he wants to go with his nerves still intact, who's complaining?

a Someone with a wizened, terrified **a** tends to shrink away from adversity. He is floored by problems and setbacks – a single punch is usually enough to have him reeling on the ropes, after which he may be slow to bounce back.

a This is a script **a**, like the one you find on typewriters. Someone with a firm, upright script **a** subdues any fear and won't allow it to interfere with progress. He accepts criticism and rejection squarely and adjusts his game plan accordingly. Every comment, however damaging it may seem, is ultimately of value. This character never allows self-doubt or memories of previous bad experiences to eat away at his chances of success. By swallowing his pride and facing up to fear head-on, he usually wins through in the end.

By the way, you can always double-check a person's resilience level using a capital **N** or capital **Z**. Neither of these letters means anything special on its own, but they come in handy when you need to know whether the writer is coping well in life or buckling under the strain.

A coping **N** should be upright: N .

If it isn't, if the limbs splay out in all directions: Λ or if the construction of it is nothing but a jumbled mess: Ŋ , the pressure is beginning to show. Remember the old ques-

tion: 'If you built it out of wood, would it still stand up?'
That applies to capital **N**'s. Something as shaky as this, for
instance: $\mathcal{N}$, would drop to pieces in seconds.

A capital **Z** too should be sturdy: $\mathbb{Z}$.

If the letter is compressed: $\mathbf{z}$, or leaning too far
back: $\mathbf{z}$, or just in a general state of disarray: $\mathbf{z}$, take it
as a sign that all is not well, that current problems are pressing down on the writer to such an extent that they colour his
whole outlook on life, preventing him from exploring his
full potential; he may be struggling to keep his show on the
road.

Other **a**'s to look out for

a **(Recoiling)** This person has had a run of narrow
escapes or near misses in life. These have left
him weak and vulnerable, unable to take much
more. He fears anything else going wrong and
does not have the strength of character to cope
with a disaster or serious downturn in his affairs.

a **(Incomplete a with hole in top)** A sign of
gullibility. He listens far too much to what other
people say and not enough to his own intuition.

a **(Strong face, short stem)** A real tough individual. The toughness is a front, of course, but it
makes him defiant, bull-headed, determined, and
someone who sees his plans right through to the
end.

Prejudice

C, c

C's big and small tell us two things: on the positive side, how eager a person is to learn new things, not just about himself but also about the world around him; and on the negative side, how fixed are his views, how strong his prejudices.

The letter **C** is really about open-mindedness – the willingness to take fresh information and different opinions at face value, without filtering them through a mesh of prejudices and long-held, outmoded viewpoints first.

On the whole, the deeper and plumper the **C**, the greater will be the writer's appetite for the new, the novel and the interesting.

A **C** this size means that the writer's mind is wide open. He is constantly monitoring the news on all fronts. Furthermore, he will process what he discovers quickly and approach the latest advances or changes, plus any expansive experiences, with a positive attitude. The larger the **C** and the greater the space inside it, the more interested (and interesting) the writer will tend to be.

C   The thinner and weaker the **C** becomes, the less fired-up a writer will be by the world about him. Cursed by the twin demons of apathy and indifference, he will neither seek knowledge actively, nor have a great ability to retain it when it arrives. Sometimes this can be put down to a poor memory. Other times, it's because he is too caught up in his own concerns, preferring to let the rest of the world carry on without his active participation.

C   A **C** with a slight inward curl or hook on it means the writer has a number of beliefs or perspectives which are deeply-felt and unshakeable. For instance, Mr Hooked-**C** may believe that all politicians are ruthless, power-hungry hypocrites, forever on the make; as a result, when he hears the news that a member of the Government is opening a new shelter for the destitute, he will fail to see any positive aspects to the gesture and will *automatically* write off the whole operation as cheap propaganda and a bid for votes.

The prejudice may be political or religious, or consist of a series of leftover opinions and perspectives from his upbringing. They may not always be set in concrete, but will be difficult to shake off all the same. The greater the curl, the more ingrained his attitudes.

C   When that curl becomes a pocket inside the **C**, you may well be staring at prejudice of the severest kind. In more extreme cases this could even border on outright bigotry: racism, homophobia, sexism, etc. Or else it may amount to a blind antipathy to specific ideas or groups: men with beards, Communism, a certain football team, or whatever.

$\mathcal{C}$ A filled-in pocket is the sign of a mind so closed that to confront it with a contradictory viewpoint is probably to invite an assault on your person. The writer looks out on the world with unseeing eyes and a fixed perspective which remains unyielding despite overwhelming evidence to the contrary.

NB: Bigotry is a serious accusation to level at anyone, so do check with other signs elsewhere in the writing before making your judgement.

$\mathcal{C}$ A simple loopy **C** belongs to someone who is cautious and who thinks just a little too much about every possible repercussion before allowing himself to indulge in a new venture. He hesitates and dawdles until he is absolutely sure that the information he is receiving is correct, by which time it may be too late to take advantage of it anyway.

Openness to Fresh Experience

G

> If **C**'s reveal an appetite for information, then the capital **G** must be its twin brother, since embodied in this single letter is the writer's hunger for fresh and interesting experiences.

The likeness may be no coincidence. After all, what is a **G** but a **C** with a strange-shaped tail on it: $\mathcal{G}$?

An open **G**, thrown wide like a gaping mouth, belongs to someone who is driven by a desire for stimulation – exotic foods, new cars, different and interesting places – someone who wants to live fast and long, packing into his life as much as he possibly can. He craves change and excitement and is loath to judge an experience before he's had a go at it himself.

This is a **G** for lesser, more retiring souls. Narrower and tighter with little room for new experience, this person will not welcome change or a rapid pace of life, and is likely to have an overall backward slant to his handwriting. If things move too quickly before he is ready, he becomes nervous and could dig in his heels in an effort to slow the whole process down.

Here the mouth of the **G** is closed, taking the writer's mind with it. New horizons may beckon, but they'll seldom be explored. The Closed-**G** individual is a committed reactionary who would fight to the death to maintain the status quo.

Between the wide-open mouth and the tight-shut mouth lies a kind of halfway house, where the **G** is semi-closed and seems to be balancing a small tray between its jaws. Such an individual is not averse to trying new things, but does so more selectively. He is quite guarded, preferring to pick and choose such activities rather than indulging himself wholesale, and thereby risking disappointment, discomfort or embarrassment.

Pockets, as with **C**'s, signify prejudice of some kind, though not of the racist or homophobic sort, more along the lines of 'once bitten, twice shy'.

A **G**-pocket means that the writer nurtures reservations about a whole range of issues. Consequently he is often too cautious, too sensible even, which prevents him enjoying to the full any new opportunity on offer. Often the blame for restrictive attitudes rests on the shoulders of parents. All those solemn warnings in childhood: 'Don't do that, you'll catch cold', 'You mustn't try this, it's bad for you', 'God will punish you for your sins...' and so on, may now be taking their toll, so that a potential bogeyman lurks around every corner.

A loop which seems to be pulling the jaws of the **G** open from the back is a sign that the person is haunted by unsettling memories from the distant past which still cast a long shadow over choices he makes today. A strict upbringing, a string of failed relationships, a few bad experiences when a daring adventure went horribly wrong and he got hurt ... such memories run deep in the unconscious mind, confusing him about which experiences to try and which to leave alone. The end result: uncertainty, vulnerability and an inability to make free, unbiased choices.

As a back-up to the letter **G**, or if you can't find one on the page but would still like to gauge the writer's appetite for fresh experiences, then look for a capital **U**.

The size, width and depth of the **U** can be a handy guide to someone's lust for life. If the **U** is large and open with a lot of capacity inside: $\mathcal{U}$, the person who wrote it, too, will possess that sort of attitude when it comes to adventure, fun and experimenting with different approaches and pursuits. A tight **U**: $\mathcal{U}$, on the other hand, leaves little room for new experiences at all; while someone who draws a low chunky **U**: $\smile$ likes to be a jack of all trades and sample a little bit of everything. He will have a mind packed with trivia, but ask him to explain almost anything in depth and he'll give you a blank look. 'Depth? What's that, then?'

Stubbornness

S, s

Stubbornness is a close ally of blind prejudice. Both are founded on the preconceived notion that one particular approach is the correct one, and that all other approaches must therefore be wrong. And just as prejudice can be found in the top loop on a **C** or **G**, so stubbornness is indicated by the curl on the letter **S**.

To begin with, a free-thinking **S** looks like this: S .

Here the writer expresses his opinions freely but is also prepared to give contrary viewpoints a fair hearing. Well-reasoned arguments receive positive responses and nothing is dismissed out of hand.

If the bottom of the **S** curls around sharply before slashing its way across to the next letter, then the person concerned is not afraid to put his view in the furtherance of getting his own way. He will choose the perfect moment to say his piece and expect to receive a positive answer in return. If he does not, he will argue fiercely or slink away, temporarily defeated, only to return tomorrow with the same demand couched in different language. He doesn't give up easily.

If the bottom of the **S** swoops back over the top of it, then this writer too is used to getting what he wants. The difference is that, if you don't give it to him, he will try every trick in the book to get his own way by other means. From the moment you say no, you will need to keep your wits about you. His determination knows no bounds and, however long it takes, he will expect to win in the end.

When the **S** appears to be crouching uneasily with a stiff neck, there is a severe reluctance to take on board any further facts or information. This guy isn't stubborn, he's just wary or sceptical and will not accept what is told to him without a good deal of persuasion.

The real problems start, though, when you spot a hook on the front of an **S**. It invariably means that the writer has a tendency to be blinkered about certain issues. He approaches life with a set of established rules and values already in place, and tends to dismiss anything which does not fall in with what he already believes. When challenged he will stand his ground as a pre-set response, rather than thinking matters through afresh.

When that hook twists into a distinct curl, you know immediately that the writer can be extremely obstinate when he wants to be. You may try to argue with him and express an entirely reasonable point of view, but once his mind is made up he's unlikely to give an inch and will press on and do what he believes to be right, irrespective of what those around him might say.

Slightly more of a challenge than the curly **S** is the bullish **S**. See the way its head is bent low, as though ready to charge? Nothing will stop this character: he is fixed in purpose, direct in manner and is going to barge through every obstacle in his path until he has achieved what he set out to do.

The opposite to the above is the Eager Snail. This occurs at the end of a word and belongs to someone who is very interested in making headway in life and always curious about what lies beyond the horizon, yet is held back constantly by a host of pressing responsibilities. As time goes by these may lighten, so freeing him to make greater strides. For now, though, he is stuck where he is, anticipating what is to come, but unable to do very much towards hastening its arrival.

Privacy/Secrecy

n

> A small **n** unlocks the private side of your personality,
> the part of you which is kept hidden, well away from
> prying eyes, and reveals how open and up-front
> you can be.

We all have secrets – feelings, fears, regrets, beliefs, pangs
of guilt; some run so deep that we don't even feel safe telling
them to our loved ones or closest friends. Instead, as we discovered earlier, we pack them away to the very back of our
mind in the hope that they won't return to trouble us.

For many people the desire for privacy is an end in itself,
a natural extension of their personality. They have a public
side which they share with the world – in restaurants, at
work, during parties – and then a deeper, more personal
side, a world of thoughts and memories, wishes and dreams
to which everyone else is denied access.

An **n** is made up of two elements – a short stem: and a
hoop: $\cap$. The writer's Secrecy Factor is measured by how
far the hoop rises up the stem. The bigger the hoop, the
more likely the individual is to have a very private side to
his character.

n   On a private **n** the hoop and the stem tend to be the same size. This conceals a storehouse of sensitive details behind a door marked: 'STRICTLY PRIVATE. KEEP OUT'. The writer is an extremely reserved person and, at times, may well be secretive simply for the sake of it, much to the consternation of all the gossips around him, keen to know what he knows.

ʰ   By contrast, a shamelessly public person will draw his **n** in this curiously flattened way, with hardly a hoop at all – just a stem and acres of space. Such an individual has little worth hiding. He is upfront about most aspects of his life and keeps nothing back. Any stories he has to tell will be flaunted mercilessly before the public gaze and no doubt fleshed out into something far more than they actually are, for greater impact.

ŋ   This **n**, with its defensive tail, tells us that the writer has, in truth, very little to be private about, but he doesn't see it that way. Whatever his secret is, he is terrified that it might leak out, and so has mounted a rearguard action to protect it.

Many people do this. Fearing that others might cheat to catch a glimpse of what they're hiding, they erect a shield of cleverly thought-out lies and exaggerations and other devious ploys, all designed to blur the edges of the truth and keep the nosier of Nosy Parkers at bay.

ŋ   Here, where the tail extends downward, the writer nurses a fear of divulging the truth bordering on paranoia. To protect his secrets he has thrown together a series of barriers and deceits, hurdles and untruths so elaborate that even Indiana Jones would find them impregnable.

Personal Fulfilment

h

> This letter mirrors all your innermost desires for balance, well-being and contentment. Are you growing, learning and changing, or merely clinging to the status quo? The **h** knows, making it a sort of spiritual weathervane.

Just as **M**'s relate to fulfilment within relationships, and double **l**'s tell us how fulfilled you are in your work, so it falls to the **h** to represent the whole you. Look on it as a progress marker, if you like, measuring how far down the spiritual road you have come and how much you have learned along the way.

By rights, an **h** should consist of a well-proportioned, upright stem: / with a hoop: ∩ nudging up cosily alongside it. The degree of fulfilment is gauged by how much space is contained within the hoop and how far it creeps up the side of the stem.

So...

ከ A hoop that is buoyant with plenty of room inside shows that the writer is, for the most part anyway, pleased with the way life is unfolding.

There may be room for improvement – isn't there always?
– but he has a strong set of values and an understanding of
what good living is all about. Things are going well.

h   An overblown hoop is often not quite such a posi-
     tive sign. If all the handwriting has a distinct
     'Toytown' look to it, it signifies innocent plea-
sures and a fun, uncomplicated character. If, on the other
hand, the bloated **h**-loop turns up in ordinary writing, the
individual concerned will be putting on a show of happiness
and contentment which is not for real. Inside he is stewing
over negative experiences in the past, so any feelings of fulfilment will be short-lived.

An **h** with a hoop so flat that it is barely a hoop at all belongs to someone who has restricted his own potential for personal growth. He lacks spirit and gusto, and although a certain desire for enlightenment may be present, his steps towards it are faltering. Progress can only be made when based on greater faith and trust and an understanding that life is about change, movement, risk, metamorphosis and challenge, not hesitation, fear or a dedication to preserving the status quo.

Often you will run up against someone who claims to be deeply religious and at one with life and the Universe – 'Like, sure, yeh, I'm a deeply spiritual person' – yet who also has a shrivelled hoop on his **h**. One can put this down to the deep-seated fear of someone who has taken refuge in religion because he feels insecure and unable to cope alone. He has faith in God but no faith in himself.

Other **h**'s to look out for

(**Tall stem, tiny hoop**) Aspirations, plenty of potential, but selling himself short. Adverse circumstances plus, in all likelihood, a large dose of fear are preventing him from realizing his dreams.

(**Blossoming hoop disconnected from stem**) Plenty of useful experience but for its own sake; it has not contributed to spiritual growth, merely to general knowledge. Provides confidence, not understanding.

(**Small stem, flat loop**) Too many small interests; fails to set one overriding achievable goal. Will not begin to grow until he learns to focus on what he wants *specifically*.

(Loopy stem, small hoop) Limited vision, coupled with fear of change and a deep desire to blend in with the crowd. Afraid of failure.

 (Cramped hoop hunched up against the stem) Lack of daring. May be scared of success or taking risks. Past failures are a trip-wire.

Joie de Vivre

Y

Capital **Y** is about spirit and enthusiasm – and whether
the writer enjoys life, appreciates its value and takes full
advantage of all the wonderful experiences on offer.

To enjoy life to the full we require happiness, harmony and
balance in equal measure.

Equipped with all three, we can tackle even the most
adverse circumstances with confidence and a quiet expectation of winning through. Without them, our everyday
world becomes a relentless round of obstacles and setbacks
instead of opportunities and openings. Joy
is vital. If there is no joy in a person's
heart he will grow older faster and always
seem to be disenchanted with what he has,
forever teetering on the brink of gloom, frustration, anger, depression or any one of a
dozen other common ills.

A positive, strong **Y** stands tall with its
arms thrust excitedly into the air. It exudes

happiness and positivity, vitality and ... yes, joy. If the
writer has a **Y** like that one, he is definitely on the right
track. Indeed, my advice is: whoever he is, stick with him,
because something amazing may happen at any minute.

A person's capacity to enjoy himself is embodied in the
confidence and stretch of those arms.

A modest stretch indicates moderation – someone who takes a bit of everything but will never
go the full distance. Nothing wrong in that, provided he doesn't let too much common sense get in the way
of a good time.

Something big, stiff and disjointed means an
immature person who can be over-indulgent at
times and doesn't really appreciate the value of
what he does. Many of the finer benefits of being alive are
wasted on him, frankly.

If the **Y**'s stem is kicked adrift, the writer is not
a strong person inside. He may have emotional
problems and use his social activities as a crutch
so that he doesn't have to face up to the reality of how he
truly feels.

Needless to say, anything small and wizened or
buckled and bowed is not so good. In each
instance the writer seems to have lost sight of
what real enjoyment and happiness are. He needs to expand
his realm of activities right away: meet new friends, get
drunk, visit a sauna, dance in a night-club till three in the
morning or try running naked along a beach somewhere at
dawn ... *anything* to shake him up and put a bit of pep in his
step before it's too late.

Y's after the event

The Telltale Alphabet – Summary

V: Sexual prowess – good in bed?   152
W: Enthusiasm   177
X: Fidelity and commitment in relationships   150
Y: Joie de vivre   233
Z: Resistance to pressure   217

a: Resilience   215
b: Contentment – possessions and territory   194
d: Temper   111
e: Humour   98
f: Image and fun: spotting the party animal   125
g: Anger   105
h: Personal fulfilment   229
i: Vision and foresight   184
j: Praise   203
l: Achieving goals   169
ll: Fulfilment at work   172
n: Privacy/secrecy   227
p: Optimism   191
q: Sensitivity to criticism   209
r: Concentration   179
t: Passion, honour, integrity   130, 182
th: Partnerships   144
to: Taking charge   174
tt: The secret you   147
u: Meeting people/gregariousness   122
w: Defensiveness   213
y: Responsibility   161
z: Criticism and judgement   206

The Telltale System in Action

Having dealt in great detail with the Telltale letters individually, we must now move on and see how the System works in operation.

For this you'll need a piece of handwriting – preferably by somebody you know quite well. That way, you can check off the signs one by one and be sure that you are right.

Any piece of scribble will do, although if you cast your mind back a few chapters you may recall how the words 'Elvis Presley' proved to be an interesting way of testing out the System. Or better still, 'Elvis Aaron Presley – the King of Rock 'n' Roll'. From those eight and a half short words you will be able to pull together a fairly comprehensive list of the writer's main attributes.

If there are certain specific items of information you are keen to know about a person, then pick a phrase containing as many of the appropriate Telltale letters as possible.

So, for example, to discover more about the state of someone's marriage, you need a piece of writing containing the letters: **E**, **m**, **th**, **H**, and **v** ('Expect me in Hanover this Wednesday'?). If you are about to hire an extra pair of hands to help you around the office, then I suggest something made up mostly of **E**'s, **r**'s, **R**'s, **I**'s, **i**'s, **c**'s, **to**'s, **l**'s and **B**'s ('Bill and I decided to tickle Eric Robson till he cried'), and you can also throw in any other letter which answers specific questions you may have about that person.

To illustrate how the letters work together, a friend of mine, Jim, a freelance radio producer, is going to write out a random phrase for us to examine.

In less than six days I own

There.   *Eak Cart!*

Nine words in all. Not much to go on, you might think; but taking each letter both individually and in relation to its neighbours and interpreting them all according to the rules laid down in the Alphabet, you can collect large amounts of information about Jim – much of it very personal and private.

Suddenly, I bet he wishes he hadn't offered to help.

THE OVERALL LOOK

First of all, from the regular spacing between words, we know that he is systematic in his approach to any task he undertakes, a man who gets things done. And because the writing is horizontal, rather than drifting upward or downward across the page, we know that this is someone who is neither pessimistic nor optimistic. His expectations are fairly well-balanced.

Also, judging by the way the letters swirl around each other and are sometimes joined together top and bottom, Jim is a speedy thinker who is able to translate his ideas into action very quickly. (He jotted down this phrase in a couple of seconds, without thinking.)

Finally, since the words are upright and not heavily embroidered with a thousand loops and kinks, we can readily assume that the man is sane, straightforward and untroubled by painful episodes from the past. There are no brakes holding him back. Wherever he plans to go in life, whatever he hopes to achieve, he has the wherewithal to make it.

THE WORDS INTERPRETED

As always, we begin by isolating the capital **E**, as in Earl's Court: $\mathcal{E}$.

Note how all three cross-bars are connected firmly to the stem. This is a good sign. But see also how the head-line at the top is so long that it stretches right over the word, pulling the rest of the **E** with it. Altogether, this means that Jim is primarily an ideas man. He lives in the world of concepts and innovation and enjoys putting these across to others. Indeed, he can be very persuasive, even overbearing at times, when conveying his thoughts and beliefs.

The heart-line is short which means that the expression of deeper loving emotions is not his strong point, and because it is connected to the head-line by a small thin diagonal slash: $\mathcal{E}$, we know that he diverts much of his emotional energy into his ideas.

The sex-line is healthy, so Jim is no stranger to sexual activity! More than that I had better not say.

Now we go back to the beginning of the sentence and examine the letters one by one.

In   The **I** is strong and bold, so he is independent, firm, decisive and makes his mark confidently.

The **n** is fairly closed so Jim has a private side to

him which he likes to keep well-hidden.

leas. His **l** is strong too, and a good size – so he has
sensible ideas which he is happy to suggest
because he knows them to be workable. He never
overreaches his capabilities.

The **e** is jolly with a bright smile, so Jim has a
great personality. He certainly likes a laugh.

The two **s**'s provide the first sign of a problem.
The first is closed with a loop, showing that he
can be extremely stubborn once he digs his heels
in. He knows what he wants and if he's sure he is
right, he will hang on in there until he gets it.

The second **s** is smarter. It shows that he also
approaches tasks with a readiness to learn and a
certain eagerness to get started.

than The **t** projects energy. Clearly, when Jim decides
to go for a goal, he gives it everything he's got,
merging sexual energy with his heart and intellectual energies to produce a powerhouse of
effort and enthusiasm. The cross-bar on the **t** is a
little high, showing that he is not too comfortable
with deep emotional issues and adopts a rational
approach to such matters in case he is perceived
as weak or cissy. Consequently, as shown by the
th, he is linked to his partner more on a mental
level than intensely emotionally.

Taking the **h** separately and relating it to him, he
is quite fulfilled as a person, but only by the

number of experiences he has clocked up. The hoop of the **h** is kept very separate from the stem, showing that he is not spiritually fulfilled. If he were, the hoop would be rising up alongside the stem.

The **a** looks strong and bold and, despite the small loop in the stem displaying a slight nervousness at the back of his mind, he is not one to dwell on life's ups and downs. He prefers to go for what he wants and tackle problems as they arrive. He is very resilient.

This **n**, unlike the first, displays a far greater openness. Note this contradiction as it shows a different side to his character – private, but accessible too.

Another stubborn **s**, but also with a slash across to the **i**. He is not afraid to go for what he wants. Since the **i** seems to be backward-sloping, as though the slash on the **s** is dragging it back, this means that whenever he lets his requirements be known, he expects other people to do what he asks and make it happen. He can be demanding at times.

There is no dot on the **i**, so he clearly sees many perspectives at the same time, rushing about, able to get a firm grip on several diverse issues one after the other.

The **x** is non-committal and a warning that, although Jim may seem willing and able to make a firm commitment to his partner, somewhere behind that promise is a feeling of losing his freedom. He may be hard to pin down.

The stem of the **d** is bent over into a scorpion's tail, though a mild one, so he does lose his temper and is capable of issuing vicious put-downs; but because this tail has a loop in it, he clearly tries to bite his tongue whenever possible, rather than risk hurting or alienating people. Much of his anger probably gets worked off by other means – such as playing squash or tennis.

Another resilient **a**, slightly larger this time, so he may be a little defensive and a touch too forceful when trying to get his own way. Often he pushes things somewhat too far and goes out on a limb.

The **y** has a fairly deep cradle, showing that he knows how to enjoy his daily life and is buoyant and fun. The tail is another sign of low commitment. Whatever responsibilities may be thrown at him, in his heart he would prefer to be a free agent and not tied down: a master rather than a servant.

Another stubborn **s**, quite fierce and almost bullish, so again, once he knows what he wants, he is likely to charge through all obstacles until he makes it a reality.

Another confident **I**, well-spaced from the other letters.

owu   A nice round **o**, showing that he is open, generous and can be quite sensitive when he wants to
be, although the small pocket inside the **o** means
he has reservations about being too giving. His
generosity will probably be selective. He is no
fool evidently.

The **w** is a little defensive, with a bulbous right
arm. On one side it is pulling the **o** in, and on the
other it has a hold of the **n**, so he is used to co-
ordinating people and being at the centre of operations. If challenged, he may start justifying
himself rather fiercely.

The **n** is another open and accessible one, con-
firming what we already know.

Eatk   The **E** we have dealt with already.

This third **a** has a small loop in the stem and suggests a little more anxiety than before, a greater
depth of thought, more worry. Although Jim
claims to be about to own Earl's Court, maybe
the very mention of it is enough to bring on fears
and apprehension.

A very open nosy **r** that could only belong to
someone with a highly-tuned radar for what is
going on around him. He is filled with curiosity
and is eager to take on board as much information as possible. The stem of the **r** is virtually
non-existent, so his interest in things has a scat-
ter-gun feel to it, rather than coming from a position of inner strength and a need to know. He

learns details for their own sake.

The **l** is tied firmly to the **r** behind it. Note the strong connection, forming a streak which pulls it back. Because the **l** is a stem pure and simple, the top of it relates to the mind (as with the **E** and all other stems). Altogether, then, this means that events in the past fuel Jim's aspirations. He probably brings many years of experience to what he does, and this expertise prevents him thinking unrealistically and keeps him grounded. (A difficult formation, this, so let's not dwell on it for too long.)

The **s** leans back and is quite open, indicating an objectivity which he brings to his work; his judgement is probably very sound, again based on experience. This contrasts with the earlier stubborn **s**'s, and marks yet another facet of his nature.

The **C** is bulbous, very round and tall with plenty of room inside for fresh information. He has a huge appetite for knowledge, but because the top of the **C** is hooked over we know that Jim also harbours a number of prejudices. Once again, this may be put down to experience. He has lived a lot and must therefore bring a number of preconceptions to any job he tackles. Of course, it may denote something more serious and that should be borne in mind.

A round **o**, as we saw above, means a high degree of openness, sensitivity and generosity.

But because it has a small pocket inside it where the **C** loops around, this trait is slightly qualified: he has reservations about giving too much.

The **u** in 'Court' is of the best kind: wide open, joining together the letters on either side of it and indicating that Jim enjoys meeting people and socializing and interacting with them.

Another curious, gossipy **r** that looks up and is very aware of what is going on around it. The stem is split, however, so there is a bit of confusion here. Standards set in childhood obviously have a bearing on his behaviour. He may have been taught, when he was very young, to keep himself to himself, but has developed in quite the opposite direction as he has grown up. Unconsciously, he still feels slightly guilty.

A somewhat flighty **t**. The cross-bar slashes across the stem midway, showing again that he carries out tasks with conviction and believes firmly in what he does.

SUMMARY

So, taking Jim's personality as a whole, we know he is a nice guy, very dynamic, with plenty of ideas which he expresses with great force.

He believes passionately in what he does and sets realistic targets which he achieves by firing up other people with his enthusiasm. He is able to act alone and make decisions confidently; he is an achiever, a quick-thinker, with a short temper which he manages to keep in check, except when his ideas are challenged, when he will fight quite hard to justify what he believes in.

Pleasant, amiable, open, moderately generous, good to socialize with, but not confident on a deep emotional level. Sex is a huge attraction for him, but the expression of true love makes him feel a little uncomfortable. His partner accepts him for his mind and personality rather than his depth.

And all that from just nine short words jotted down in a hurry!

CONTRADICTIONS

Despite the fact that several versions of the same letter appear here, each providing what seems like contradictory information, that does not mean there is a conflict. You are merely witnessing different sides of the writer's personality.

A stubborn **s** and an easy-going **s** are not incompatible. The person may well be easy-going most of the time, and yet on certain issues dear to his heart he becomes obstinate in the extreme. He will be pushed so far and no further. Similarly, it is not unusual to find an open **n** and an extremely private **n** in the same writing. The writer is simply letting it be known that when the time comes to be accessible and engaging and show his personality, he can do it very well. But he also has a few secrets which he likes to protect. He treasures time spent alone with his private thoughts and there are certain aspects of him which he will not share with anyone.

What the 'Jim' example demonstrates is the way that letters can be interpreted, not only in isolation but also in relation to their neighbours.

In particular, whenever an **s** or a **w**, or indeed any other
letter which can signify 'asking for what you want and getting your own way', appears to be dragging the letter next
to it backwards, as the **s** does with the **i** in 'six': $\mathcal{SUX}$ you
know that the writer imposes his views on others and likes
giving orders. In extreme instances it may even amount to
bullying, though not in Jim's case.

Earlier on, when we were exploring the Alphabet, we saw
the way the cross-bar of a **t** often overhangs the **h** next to it:
$\mathcal{th}$, meaning that the writer is forceful in the communication of his feelings and tends to be overbearing with his
partner. Similarly with a capital **F**: if the top bar extends out
too far so that it overshadows the rest of the word $-\mathcal{Fav}-$
this person will have strong opinions and plenty of ideas
which he will expect to have accepted without complaint or
query. And when the bottom half of a capital **B** nudges up
against the next letter: $\mathcal{Bav}l$, it is telling you that the writer
steams ahead to get things done, imposing on people, nudg-
ing, cajoling, even impelling them into doing what he says.

From the Alphabet you will recall that there are many
more instances too where the imposition of one letter on
another represents a person who imposes himself on
another. In other cases, for a letter to lean back weakly so
that it is almost resting on the letter behind it, as it does
here: $\mathcal{cav}$ and here: $\mathcal{stop}$ gives an indication that, at times,
the writer tends to place too much reliance on others and
will not stand up for himself.

The trick is to treat each letter as a character, an individual,
that deserves to have its say. Note what it is telling you,
then move on to the next and decipher that. At the end, tot
up the results in the same way you might tot up a grocery
bill, into one overall portrait.

ELVIS LIVES

Way back, towards the beginning of the book, if you recall, I boasted freely that, using this system, we could deduce a staggering thirteen clear facts about a person from the way he wrote 'Elvis Presley', and an even more staggering *twenty-seven* facts from: 'Elvis Aaron Presley – the King of Rock 'n' Roll'.

Well, perhaps the time has come to prove it.

I've badgered a couple more of my friends, Rebecca (a marketing consultant) and Sally (a freelance journalist and broadcaster), into taking part in a little experiment, and they have each written out one of these phrases. If you want to play along by trying to work the meanings out for yourself, then just cover up the list of interpretations with a strip of card and compare them later.

REBECCA

Elvis Presley

Portrait

First, take a look at the **E**.

Because it resembles a figure 3 written back to front, we know that Rebecca is a Showbiz type; her emotions are upfront and life tends to be some kind of performance. She is constantly on show, has a strong head-line and an even stronger sex-line, whilst her heart-line is rather too short. You would therefore expect Rebecca to be bubbly and bright and also perhaps a little theatrical and superficial.

The hook on the head-line suggests that she has fixed ideas and can be closed-minded on certain issues. Make a note to check this with an **s** later on.

Finally, because the writing has a gently-sloping upward gradient to it, we can take it that Rebecca is an optimist by nature and, since the words are well-spaced too, she is also clear-headed and takes a systematic approach to whatever she does in life.

Focusing on the remaining letters now:

The **l** is strong but very tall. This means she is confident and bold, but not all her aspirations are practical or realizable. She dreams a bit too much and needs to float back down to earth a little more often.

The **v** is strong but the thighs are not very wide, so she performs well sexually, though in a conventional way. She would never indulge in anything too tacky. The slight hook on the right thigh of the **v** indicates that she can be a real flirt at times. And, since the **v** is not connected to the letters around it, but stands alone, we must take it that sex is considered a pleasurable bodily function rather than a reason for living.

The **i** is strong too, with the dot perched immediately above the stem. From this we know that Rebecca is extremely focused on what she is doing when she is doing it. She takes one day at a time and squeezes a lot into it. Tomorrow can take care of itself, and the past, well . . . forget it.

The **s** is very stubborn. This woman knows what she wants and is fixed enough in her intentions to go and get it. She may not listen to reason when her mind is made up and hates being told that she is wrong. Reprimands constitute a real affront to her sensibilities.

Such a nosy **P**. Look at the snout on that! Here we have a real busybody. To a certain extent, she is nosy in order to find out what is going on and protect her interests. But there is also a whole load of gratuitous curiosity thrown in too. Owing to the shape of the **P**, we can deduce that she can occasionally be a little snooty. Not much, nothing too alarming – but it's there.

The **r** looks downward so, again, she is able to concentrate and keep her mind on the job when the situation demands it.

The **e** is happy and smiley indicating a warm personality.

Another extraordinarily stubborn **s** here. And a slash across to the **l**, showing that she has the guts to ask for what she wants and expects to get it.

A different sort of **l**, revealing a more thoughtful side. There is a lot going on in her brain, and she often reins in her adventurous, idealistic side in favour of being cautious and contemplative.

Another laughing **e** – maybe this one is laughing *too* much! She probably hates to be serious for long, and would prefer to have a good time and enjoy every minute of the day.

y   The **y** suggests another free spirit. She hates over-committing herself and would prefer someone else to worry about paying the mortgage and the other bills, leaving her to spread her wings and fly. She has a real lust for life, though occasionally, as the loop indicates, she is prevented from being too wild by deeper feelings of duty which she has grown up with and which still rest on her shoulders.

And there you have it. I promised thirteen facts but you can see that, from just two words, we have pulled out a lot more.

The final example goes the whole hog with 'Elvis Aaron Presley – the King of Rock and Roll'. This time I will put together a general portrait of the writer's personality rather than a letter-by-letter breakdown. Refer back to the Alphabet and see if you can pinpoint all the different elements in the writing.

SALLY

Elvis Aaron Presley –
the King of Rock and Roll

Portrait

Sally is quite a strong and spirited woman, someone who is in touch with her feelings and not afraid to show them (**E**). She enjoys sex, but has certain minor inhibitions about it and is most definitely not one to swing from the lampshades during intercourse. Like Rebecca she indulges in the sex act for its own sake rather than experimenting with the wider possibilities. She could afford to let herself go more (**V**).

She is blessed with a lively mind and has a keen interest in what is going on around her (**r**), although she does tend to sell herself short intellectually, always opting for the easy route rather than exploring and exploiting her full capabilities (**stem of E and top cross-bar**). She is also rather pessimistic and can't prevent herself from expecting the worst (**downward slope of writing**). However, to her credit, she is very practical and keeps her aspirations to a realistic level (**l**).

Most times, Sally is ready for anything and enjoys being where the action is (**first s**). As shown by the **i** in Elvis, she has her mind on many things simultaneously, with her attention roaming all over the place. She can be a little stubborn when the mood takes her (**second s**), and although she manages to appear relaxed on the surface there is a certain amount of anxiety present, particularly in her outlook and behaviour – perhaps as a product of a strict upbringing. Again, in this respect, she needs to let herself go a little more (**A**).

Over the years she has developed a certain resilience, but this is very much on the surface. Underneath, she has all sorts of confusing thoughts which prevent her being as confident and tough as she'd like to be (**loopy a**). In many ways she is actually quite a shy and private person (**n**) who often fakes a cheery disposition in order to make herself more acceptable (**first e in Presley**).

She is interested in people rather than being fanatically curious about their lives. Again, her upbringing has something to do with this. Perhaps she has been taught by her parents not to poke her nose into other people's affairs, and this advice has stayed with her to this day (**P with top of** nose connected back to base of stem).

Her aspirations tend to need firming up by other people
(**the l in Presley strongly supported by the s behind it**);
she requires support and encouragement as a matter of
course. But on the whole Sally is someone who enjoys life
(**cradle on y**) and would enjoy it more if she were able to
free herself from the rules and guidelines laid down in her
childhood (**loop in the same y**). She has a certain number
of responsibilities to contend with, though nothing she can't
handle (**tail on y**).

So far, this information has been gleaned from the words
'Elvis Aaron Presley'. How are you doing? Have you managed to keep up?

Let's move swiftly on and reach the end.

Sally operates intuitively with a great sense of caring and
compassion, and enjoys helping others along the road (**t in
the**). She is more fulfilled, personally and spiritually, than
many people, and would be even more so if only she were
able to break free from outdated and restrictive thought-pat-
terns and dare to take more risks (**h in the**).

She can be very affectionate, and quite persuasive when
she wants something done, almost to the point of bullying
others into compliance, although they are unlikely to notice
since she makes her moves gently and quietly (**K**).

She enjoys being entertained and can be great fun when
she is drawn out, but she needs to be with the right sort of
crowd to really shine (**f in of**). There is a private, shy side
to her personality (**n in King**). She is likely to get very
angry quite often (**angry g in King**), but the anger is stored
up rather than vented, and when it does leak out it will be
in a quick burst, then everything will go quiet again (**stem
of d**). The anger she does store up has caused the **d** in 'and'

to split almost to the top of the stem. This is a sign of duality, so maybe she wants to kick and shout and scream sometimes and show her temper, but because she is well-mannered and was told as a little girl that it wasn't polite to throw tantrums she now bottles up these feelings, putting a firm lid on them, when in fact she should set them free. She will probably walk out rather than force a confrontation.

Sally is gullible at times, and so tries to be guarded wherever possible (**a in and**). She tends to breeze innocently (**o in Roll**) through life on a wing and a prayer. Things move fast in her world, leaving her little time to plan adequately (**R in Rock**). Despite having quite an appetite for fresh and interesting information (**c in Rock**), there are a few prejudices mixed in here, fixed approaches and viewpoints which she brings to bear on everyday situations, and these colour her judgement. They are minor but they do make a difference (**Hook on c**).

On the whole she is fairly fulfilled in her work (**ll**), but could achieve a lot more.

That's about it. So how did you do, then?

This is an astonishing amount of information to glean from eight or nine words, I'm sure you'll agree. Imagine what you could do with a whole paragraph!

Note that it is not necessary to deal with the letters in the strict order in which they appear on the page. We pull out information from all over the place, building up the clues piece by piece until we have a complete portrait.

Most important of all, let me also add that the Sally analysis is advanced stuff, so if you only managed to pick up, say, 40% of the story as we went along, then you're doing pretty well. One thing is for sure: the more you practise, the better you'll become. It is really very easy and – as Jim, Rebecca and Sally will confirm – extremely accurate too.

Here's a couple more. Do as we did before: break them down letter by letter and then, when you have the various items of information you need, hone them into a sensible, readable portrait.

ELIZABETH

Elvis Aaron Presley.
The King of Rock and Roll.

PATRICK

Elvis Presley —
The King of Rock & Roll

'Excuse me, but I can't help noticing that you haven't included a section anywhere in the book about signatures. They must be quite an important factor when analysing hand-writing, or am I wrong again?'

Well ... actually, yes you are.

Many people, particularly graphologists, place a lot of emphasis on signatures and regard them as extremely important.

Since the Telltale System operates by interpreting each letter individually, if the letters in a person's signature are clear and legible, you may apply to them the same general rules that we have been discussing here. However, if the letters are mangled and utterly indecipherable, then there is little to be gained, in my view, from examining them too closely. The very fact that they are higgledy-piggledy probably speaks volumes about the writer in any case.

I do not feel that we need to devote an entire separate section to signatures – not in this book anyway. You will be able to glean more than enough information from the rest of the handwriting. In most cases, the signature is but a minor factor in the equation.

Uses for the System

The Telltale Alphabet has shown itself to have a wide range of uses, apart from the most obvious one of scrutinizing the random jottings of family and friends.

i) It gives instant access to the personality of prospective partners. This has got to be a good thing. For a start it saves time. No longer do you have to waste energy dating someone, only to find out later that he or she is completely unsuitable. A quick glance at their handwriting will reveal whether or not they are honest, kind, romantic, generous or anything else you are looking for. By the same token you can also prepare yourself for any bad points: a raging temper, meanness, a potential for manipulation or deceit. Even the most basic knowledge of the Alphabet can take you from Heartbreak City to Ecstasyville virtually overnight.

ii) Personnel selection. This system has proved its worth time and time again when it comes to choosing suitable employees. Whereas conventional handwriting techniques concentrate on very basic traits, such as reliability, versatility, focus and diligence, the Telltale Alphabet provides this information and a whole lot more. From just five or six words on a written application form, for instance, it is possible to know how well a newcomer will fit into the existing office environment; how he or she will react to criticism or direction; whether there are likely to be ugly scenes, slanging matches, bullying and temper tantrums, or whether the individual remains calm under pressure and completes jobs to time and with a high degree of skill.

Done properly, such assessments can help avoid expensive mistakes where square pegs are fitted into round holes, but also it promises a tighter control over the calibre of person appointed to a particular post.

iii) Detecting forgeries. There is nothing to rival the Telltale Alphabet when it comes to winkling out fakes and forgeries. Because it relies on emotional, sexual and mental energy as well as the traces of pain and insecurity in a writer's unconscious mind, and therefore goes right to the heart of the subject, this system makes it very difficult for anyone to obscure completely his true identity. No matter how hard he tries to confuse or distort what he writes, he will always give away some clue as to how he thinks or feels. Since handwriting is as unique as a fingerprint, it can usually be traced right back to its owner.

iv) In business negotiations the system can be used to vet the handwriting of opponents. With very little preparation, you can know their strengths and weaknesses which can then be employed as a hidden negotiating tool in your dealings with them. Sneaky, but fun!

All these are valid proven ways of putting the techniques laid out in this book to work for you. One of the most amusing uses for the system, though, has been in the interpretation of company letterheads.

v) Logos. Many businesses, particularly restaurants, prefer 'handwritten' logos to the standard printed kind, and of course this plays right into our hands. Just as theatre posters send out a very definite energy to consumers, as we discovered earlier, one that mirrors the quality of the product they are promoting, so do company logos.

When the chairman and the rest of the board pick out a particular emblem to represent their venture, they believe they are making their decision based on colour, shape, size, cost and a few other factors. And they are, to a certain extent. But there is much more to it than that. Unconsciously, they are also choosing something that represents and endorses the philosophy behind the company. The emblem, once selected, will be their badge in the marketplace, so if it is strong, eye-catching and powerful-looking, this message will be conveyed to customers and other traders and the company stands a good chance of prospering. People will have faith in it. If, on the other hand, it is weak and badly designed, if it simply doesn't feel right, then those same customers and traders will pick up on that too – again, unconsciously – and the business will not do so well.

In much the same way that an old haddock gives off an unpleasant smell, a faulty company logo gives off a bad vibe which all of us pick up on subliminally and react to.

In every case where the letters or words in the logo are designed to look handwritten, you can apply the Telltale System to them and work out what the company is *really* telling you about itself.

Take the Virgin logo, for instance:

This is packed with endearing and positive qualities, symbolizing optimism, strength, sexual presence, awareness and a free spirit.

This particular design came about, like

so many things, completely by accident. Back in 1978 Richard Branson was holding a meeting with a group of designers on his houseboat in London's Little Venice. At one point, so the story goes, he spotted someone doodling the company name on a notepad and liked it so much that he adopted it immediately; and that same design has been used ever since.

Applying the Telltale rules to it, we can see why.

To begin with, the writing slopes upward indicating an optimistic outlook, an expectation that good things will happen, which is reinforced by the steep underline beneath it.

The **V** is huge by comparison to the rest of the word, a formation usually linked with boasting wildly about sexual prowess without necessarily having the experience to back it up. In reality this **V** is very guarded, and while it has a hook at the top of the right arm which signifies a certain flirty nature, there is also a backward streak from the left arm of the **V**, meaning that teachings and experiences from the writer's upbringing are holding him back. Old standards or inhibitions prey on his mind. Therefore behind all the laddish display of sexuality lies a more apprehensive, coy individual, not so bold or experienced as he would have you believe.

The **i** shows a proper attention to the job in hand. The dot nestles fairly close to the stem, so the person keeps a keen eye on business and monitors carefully how matters are progressing.

This is confirmed by the **r** which has its head up and is therefore very aware of what is going on. It is not concentrating so much on business that it can't take in other information and watch what is happening elsewhere.

The **g** is of the 'relaxed' variety. There is no real anger trapped in it; it is gentle and forgiving and not racked with bitterness or envy or any other form of emotional upset. If anything the stem is *too* long, plunging right through the underline, emphasizing a determination to remain relaxed and have fun and not become too upset by others' behaviour.

The second **i** is like the first, except with a slightly higher dot, again illustrating the ability of the writer to keep an eye on current tasks without losing sight of the overall picture.

Finally, the **n** is enclosed and therefore private. There is a lot going on behind the scenes which is not intended for public consumption. This by no means indicates impropriety or dirty tricks, merely that the writer has a very private side and does not broadcast his every movement, feeling or decision from the rooftops.

Now, is this an accurate summing-up of the philosophy behind the Virgin company?

You bet.

Richard Branson, the man at the top, may have a reputation for never missing a PR trick to plug his latest product, but he also has a very quiet, shy, private side to which few others gain access, thereby accounting for the closed **n**.

Everything else rings true as well – the flirting, the relaxed image and approach, the fact that the **V** is extremely large, indicating plenty of bravado and bluster, when the rest of the letters are small and compact, a sign of a less flamboyant, more businesslike and serious outlook. It's all there. To my mind, it is no coincidence that the designer happened to doodle this particular design when he did, no accident that Branson spotted it and liked it, and certainly no random stroke of luck that Virgin remains today the symbol of one of Britain's most successful private companies. The positive energy of the enterprise percolates from the top down until it reaches the customers who, in turn, flock to Branson's shops, fly in his planes and wear his T-shirts. They don't know why they do, it just feels right somehow. They get a buzz from patronizing the company and being part of the Virgin image.

You can subject any 'handwritten' logo to the same scrutiny and discover the energy and motivation behind the entire company. Will it be successful in the future? Does the board of directors really know what it's doing? Is the image of the business working for or against it? The answers are in the letterhead!

These are just five possible uses for the Telltale Alphabet; I'm sure you will be able to think of dozens more.

My only request to you is that you take care. Once you have mastered the techniques set out here, they will afford you tremendous insight into the way other people function. This is a heavy responsibility and one that shouldn't be sniffed at. It is incumbent upon you not to abuse your new-found power and to make sure that you not only interpret all the signs correctly, but that you dispense any private information discreetly and sensitively.

Therefore, before you set about putting the System into practice, please bear in mind the following warnings:

1) *Be diplomatic*

People are vulnerable. As we already know, they usually take great trouble to present themselves in the best possible light and will not thank you for stripping away the rosy façade and exposing their scrupulously well-hidden thoughts and feelings to the stark light of day. So, for example, if you can see from the handwriting that a person is lousy in bed and you feel he needs to be told, then tell him privately, not in front of all his friends.

Use tact at all times. Don't embarrass anybody and, above all, *don't* go broadcasting someone's most intimate details to all and sundry.

2) *Never take no for an answer*

Some folk are so distanced from their true feelings that they won't recognize many of the things you are telling them. Women are usually very comfortable with this sort of analysis, but time and again men will listen to your interpretation of their handwriting and say, 'No, you're wrong – very wrong', which can be rather dispiriting. However, this does not mean that the Telltale System doesn't work. It merely indicates that the secrets you have uncovered – worries, fears, insecurities, old conflicts – have been tucked out of the way deliberately and for so long that the writer himself has lost touch with them. He is denying the past and wants to brush his old wounds or weaknesses under the carpet with the rest of the dirt and forget about them. And, if necessary, he should be allowed to. It's his life. Many men don't like to be seen as vulnerable and don't want to have their emotions stirred up in case they are thought of as cissy or weak. So don't go interfering where you're not wanted.

But equally don't be fobbed off – if someone says your analysis is wrong, but you are sure you're right, stick to your guns.

3) *Don't get too smug*

On the other hand if you do hear the words, 'No, you're wrong – very wrong', you should always consider the possibility that you might be.

Human behaviour comes in millions of different combinations, as does human error. On a bad day, we sometimes add five and five and get eleven. So before you become too defensive and start shouting back, 'I'm right, I'm right', run over your analysis one more time to make sure your observations are correct. Otherwise you'll only embarrass yourself, and I wouldn't want that.

4) Remember the libel laws

Don't march around with a megaphone broadcasting untruths about someone just because you think you've spotted certain unpleasant traits in his handwriting – it won't wash, I'm afraid. What you say may actually *be* true, but if the traits are well-hidden and your victim chooses to deny them, you won't have a leg to stand on when the defamation suit is served on you.

Equally, please don't use the examples given within this book as direct quotes. They're for guidance only. For instance, the fact that someone has a detached cross-bar on his **t**: , and the fact that this sign sometimes means that the person is dishonourable, cruel and even a crook, *does not always mean he is dishonourable, cruel and a crook!* Other factors must be taken into consideration as well.

You must make a full evaluation on all the evidence. Use the rough examples I have given as illustrations and for reference only – do not treat them as gospel and trot them out word for word to your subject, or at least not unless your analysis ends with the words, 'See you in court'.

As I recall, it was Jesus who said, '*Judge not, that ye be not judged.*' He had a point, and you could do worse than adopt this same phrase as your Telltale motto.

Finally, 5) Do your analysis the right way round

Simply put, you must never take a set of character traits from a particular person and then try to make them fit somehow into rules laid down within the Alphabet. This is the wrong approach entirely.

As I've said before a number of times, many people construct an outer disguise to protect their soft centre and keep their vulnerability out of harm's way. What you see on the surface may be a veneer only and have no bearing on the reality. Therefore, always study the handwriting first and apply the Alphabet to what you find; do not try to manipulate the Telltale System to fit the person. It just won't work.

In spite of the warnings, do have as much fun as you dare with the Telltale Alphabet – after all, that's what it's there for. Executed proficiently, it will provide you with hours, days, maybe even years of innocent pleasure, and all at other people's expense too!

Furthermore, in the course of your experimentation with these techniques, you may make discoveries of your own and hit upon a more refined definition of certain letters. If that's the case, please do let me know. As with all new systems, the Telltale Alphabet is a work in progress and as such is developing all the time. There is some considerable way to go yet before we understand everything about it – this book is merely the first step. So if you know something that I don't, keep me posted.

Handwritten letters only – of course!

INDEX

NOTES

NOTES